Routes out of poverty

Univer

Subject

http

E
P

Routes out of poverty

A research review

Peter Kemp, Jonathan Bradshaw, Paul Dornan,
Naomi Finch and Emese Mayhew

The **Joseph Rowntree Foundation** has supported this project as part of its programme of research and innovative development projects, which it hopes will be of value to policy makers, practitioners and service users. The facts presented and views expressed in this report are, however, those of the authors and not necessarily those of the Foundation.

Joseph Rowntree Foundation
The Homestead
40 Water End
York YO30 6WP
Website: www.jrf.org.uk

ISBN 1 85935 230 8   (paperback)
ISBN 1 85935 231 6   (pdf: available at www.jrf.org.uk)

A CIP catalogue record for this report is available from the British Library.

Cover design by Adkins Design

Prepared and printed by:
York Publishing Services Ltd
64 Hallfield Road
Layerthorpe
York
YO31 7ZQ
Tel: 01904 430033   Fax: 01904 430868   Website: www.yps-publishing.co.uk

Further copies of this report, or any other JRF publication, can be obtained either from the JRF website (www.jrf.org.uk/bookshop/) or from our distributor, York Publishing Services Ltd, at the above address.

CONTENTS

1 INTRODUCTION

Background

The Joseph Rowntree Foundation (JRF) is sponsoring a programme of research on ladders out of poverty (LOOP). As part of that initiative, the Foundation commissioned this review of the existing evidence on routes out of poverty in order to inform the shape of the programme.

There is a long history of poverty research in Britain, stretching back from the pioneering work of Seebohm Rowntree at the turn of the twentieth century, through to the *Joseph Rowntree Foundation Inquiry into Income and Wealth* (Barclay *et al.*, 1995; Hills, 1995) and the recent poverty and social exclusion survey (Gordon *et al.*, 2000). This long tradition of research has profoundly influenced our understanding of the measurement, incidence, causes and scarring effects of poverty. It has also shed much light on the ways in which people cope with their poverty on a daily basis.

A crucial feature of this research has been that it has largely been static, based on poverty at a particular moment in time. While Rowntree's seminal study uncovered the life-cycle dimension to poverty, his research and later studies were limited by the data available to cross-sectional analysis. However, in recent years, prompted by work in the USA (Bane and Ellwood, 1994) and by the development of new data such as the British

Household Panel Survey, poverty research has begun to examine the dynamic as well as the static aspects of poverty (Ashworth *et al.*, 1994; Walker and Ashworth, 1994). By looking at poverty over time, it is possible to differentiate between different poverty states, including temporary, intermittent and persistent poverty (Leisering and Walker, 1998; Walker, 1998a; Gardiner and Hills, 1999; Jenkins, 2000). This new research has helped to shift the focus of attention towards a better understanding of routes not just *into* poverty, but also, and crucially, *out* of poverty (Leisering and Leibfried, 1999).

There are a number of important reasons why it is important to examine poverty dynamics (Gardiner and Hills, 1999; Bradbury *et al.*, 2001). First, it can tell us whether poverty is an experience suffered by many people or endured by just a few. The more movement there is into and out of poverty, the greater the number of people who will be affected by it. Second, the experience of being poor is likely to be much worse for those who are poor for a long period than for those who are only briefly poor. Third, it can highlight why people are poor and what are the events that trigger movements into or out of poverty. Fourth, the design of policy instruments may need to differ according to the type of poverty experienced. For example, one-off poverty episodes may be best tackled in different ways from recurring or persistent poverty. A focus on routes out of poverty has different policy implications from a focus on routes into poverty; the latter is more concerned with the causes and prevention of poverty while the former (routes out of poverty) is more concerned with solutions to it.

The exploration of routes out of poverty has been given additional impetus by the Labour Government's commitment to tackle poverty – especially to eliminate child poverty – and social exclusion more generally (HM Treasury, 1999a, 2001). The fact that rates of child poverty are very high in Britain compared with other advanced welfare states (Bradshaw, 1999; UNICEF, 2000) makes the search for ways to tackle the problem more pressing. In addition, the growing body of evidence showing that child poverty has deleterious consequences for later life (Gregg *et al.*, 1999; Hobcraft and Kiernan, 1999; Bradshaw, 2001; Ermisch *et al.*, 2001) has served to further prompt the search for ways to help the poor to escape from their poverty.

Scope of the review

For the purpose of this review, poverty was defined to mean income poverty as well as other forms of disadvantage that result from inequality in income, wealth and opportunity. The review focuses on income poverty and income trajectories but does not cover broader questions around social mobility. Education and training are not covered in the review (except briefly in relation to young people in Chapter 4), as these were the subject of an earlier round of research in the LOOP programme.

Since 1999, the Labour Government has introduced an extensive array of measures aimed at tackling poverty and social exclusion, especially child poverty (HM Treasury, 1999a, 2001). The aim is to tackle, not only income and asset poverty, but also the wider aspects of poverty in order to ensure that children have the best possible start in life and to reduce the gap between the poorest areas and the rest. Many of these initiatives or the 'pathfinders' on which they will be based are currently being evaluated and evidence is only just beginning to emerge of their success or otherwise. In some cases, it will be many years before we can be sure whether the policy intervention actually increases lifetime opportunity or lifts successive generations out of poverty. Quite apart from issues of timing, it is not possible within the scope of one review to examine all of the policy initiatives introduced by the Government to tackle poverty.

Methods

The review is a narrative review of the literature, rather than a 'systematic review' in the sense that that term has begun to be used. The review took as its starting point the authors' existing knowledge of the literature in this area and also built on an earlier review of the drivers of social exclusion conducted for the Social Exclusion Unit (Bradshaw *et al.*, 2004). We undertook a search of relevant databases including BIDS, REGARD, SOSIG and Social Policy Net, and search engine Google. We supplemented these sources with searches of the following websites: Joseph Rowntree Foundation, Centre for the Analysis of Social Exclusion (CASE), Department for Education and Skills (DfES), Department for Work and Pensions (DWP), the Institute for Fiscal Studies (IFS) and the Social Exclusion Unit. In addition, we followed up publications cited in the list of references of the material we read. In this way, we endeavoured to encompass a wide range of literature including academic journals and books, government publications and grey literature. However, the small budget available for the work limited the amount of material that could be included in the review. Within these constraints, we have chosen to focus more on quantitative than on qualitative research evidence.

Structure of the review

This review is structured as follows. Chapter 2 summarises the evidence on poverty dynamics, looking at routes into and especially routes out of poverty. Chapter 3 focuses on the evidence about work as a ladder out of poverty. The following three chapters focus successively on young people, children and families, and older people. The final chapter identifies some important gaps in the research evidence on ladders out of poverty.

2 ROUTES INTO AND OUT OF POVERTY

This chapter reviews the evidence on poverty in Britain today. In particular, it examines movements *into* and *out* of poverty. It looks at income mobility to see whether people are poor for only a short period of their lives or whether it is a more enduring condition. It also looks at the related question of how quickly people escape from poverty and the 'trigger' factors that are associated with such exits. Finally, it looks at the extent to which people fall back into poverty after escaping from it. This chapter draws on quantitative research in order to sketch out the scale of movements into and out of poverty, and to establish the relative importance of particular routeways.

Poverty in Britain

Each year, the Department for Work and Pensions publishes a report on *Households Below Average Income* (*HBAI*), which documents the extent of low income in Britain. The *HBAI* statistics are based on disposable incomes, adjusted for household size and composition, a process known as 'equivalisation'.[1] This enables income to be notionally allocated to each individual in the household, based on the assumption that all individuals within it benefit equally from their combined income. The data is reported for *individuals* (whether adults or children) living within households having particular characteristics (for example, a couple or lone-parent household).

In this chapter, people are defined as being in poverty if they have a disposable income that is below 60 per cent of the national median.[2] This is a very commonly used measure of poverty, though other measures are available. The Government has recently devised a new approach to measuring progress towards its poverty targets (DWP, 2003c), but that is too recent for it to be reflected in research findings.

Disposable income can be measured before housing costs (BHC) are taken into account *or* after housing costs (AHC) have been deducted from incomes. Both measures have advantages and disadvantages. The after-housing costs measure is often used in poverty analyses because housing expenditure can vary considerably between and within areas for property of similar size, type and quality. Consequently, before-housing costs measures of income may overstate the living standards of households living in high housing cost localities. On the other hand, the after-housing costs measure ignores the fact that some households have chosen to pay more for better quality accommodation (DWP, 2003c). Because of data limitations, some of the literature referred to in this chapter is based only on the BHC measure. Consequently, many of the poverty statistics cited in this chapter are *before* housing costs are taken into account.

Table 1 shows the percentage of individuals with incomes below 60 per cent of the median both before and after housing costs. The data comes from the most recent *HBAI* report, which documents incomes for the year from April 2001 to March 2002. The percentage of individuals falling below the poverty line is higher on the after housing costs (22 per cent) measure than on the before housing costs one (17 per cent).

Table 1 Percentage of individuals with incomes below 60 per cent of the median, 2001/02*

	Before housing costs	After housing costs
Family type		
Pensioner couple	22	22
Single pensioner	22	22
Couple with children	16	20
Couple without children	9	11
Single with children	31	53
Single without children	16	22
Ethnic group		
White	16	20
Black Caribbean	24	35
Black non-Caribbean	29	45
Indian	21	27
Pakistani/Bangladeshi	55	63
Other	27	38
Gender and adulthood		
Children	21	30
Adult male	15	18
Adult female	17	21
Disability		
No disabled adults	15	19
1+ disabled adults	24	29
No disabled children	17	22
1+ disabled children	23	33
Tenure		
Local authority	34	48
Housing association	28	52
Private rented	19	40
Owned with mortgage	8	11
Owned outright	21	16
Other	26	18
All individuals	17	22

*Including the self-employed.

Source: DWP (2003a, Table 3.6).

One in every five individuals in Britain has an income after housing costs that is below 60 per cent of the median. Children are particularly at risk of poverty, with one in three being poor on the after housing costs measure. This is one of the highest rates of child poverty among the economically advanced nations (UNICEF Innocenti Research Centre, 2000). Adult women are more likely to be poor than adult men (21 per cent compared with 18 per cent), a finding confirmed by recent research commissioned by the Equal Opportunities Commission (Bradshaw *et al.*, 2003). Other groups of individuals that are particularly at risk of poverty include:

- lone parents

- people from minority ethnic groups

- disabled people

- social and private tenants.

Income mobility

If there is income mobility, the people who comprise the poor may change over time. As people's circumstances change over time, some people may escape from poverty. Meanwhile, other people who are not currently poor may become poor later on. Consequently, the extent of income mobility is critical to the nature of poverty. The appropriate policy response is likely to be different depending on whether the experience of poverty is a transient or persistent one (Gardiner and Hills, 1999).

Recent research on poverty dynamics has begun to reveal the extent of income mobility in Britain. In fact, there is considerable income mobility from one year to the next. The most recent *HBAI* report, for example, shows that, over the decade from 1991 to

2000, over 90 per cent of the population moved income quintile groups at least once.[3] Only 7 per cent of individuals remained in the same income quintile over this ten-year period (DWP, 2003a).

As a result of this income mobility, there is movement into and out of poverty over time. Consequently, the number of people affected by poverty is much greater than the number experiencing it at any point in time (Gardiner and Hills, 1999; Jenkins, 2000). Over the period from 1991 to 2000, half the population had a spell of poverty (DWP, 2003a).

However, most income mobility takes place over a relatively short distance. In other words, although many people move income quintile over time, they do not move very far from their 'original' quintile (Jarvis and Jenkins, 1997; Jenkins and Rigg, 2001; Burgess and Proper, 2002). For example, *HBAI* data on income mobility over the period from 1991 to 2000 shows that, where people ended up in a different quintile from where they started in 1991, they were more likely than not to finish in the adjacent quintile (DWP, 2003a). Altogether, seven out of ten people who were in the bottom quintile in 1991 were in that quintile, or the next one up, ten years later. Only one in 20 people in the bottom income quintile in 1991 ended up in the top quintile in 2000 (Table 2).

Table 2 Position in 2000 of individuals who were in the bottom quintile of the income distribution in 1991*

Position 2000	Bottom quintile in 1991 (%)
Bottom quintile	45
Second quintile	24
Third quintile	15
Fourth quintile	10
Top quintile	6
All individuals	100

*Income before housing costs.

Source: DWP (2003a, Table 7.5).

There is more movement in the middle of the income distribution than at the top or the bottom. People in the bottom end and those at the top are more likely to remain in the same income quintile than those in the middle. Over the ten years from 1991 to 2000, for example, about half of the people in the bottom and the top income quintiles remained there throughout. By contrast, those who started the period in the middle three income quintiles spent most of the period in other quintiles (DWP, 2003a).

Gardiner and Hills (1999) concluded from their analysis of income mobility that:

- people who escape from the bottom are more likely to return there than those who started with higher incomes

- the escape rates of those who stay at the bottom for more than one period seem to decline.

Persistent poverty

Some people remain poor for prolonged periods of time. Over the ten-year period from 1991 to 2000, 10 per cent of individuals who started in the bottom quintile spent the entire period there. A further 40 per cent of them spent the majority of their time there. Only 39 per cent spent the majority of this period above the bottom quintile (DWP, 2003a).

Thus, despite income mobility, there is considerable persistence in poverty among some individuals. Indeed, over the decade from 1991 to 2000, one in six individuals spent at least five years living in households below 60 per cent of median income (DWP, 2003a). Over any four years between 1991 and 2000, around a third of all individuals spent at least one year below this income threshold. Meanwhile, about one in ten people spent at least three years out of any four consecutive years during this period living in households below 60 per cent of the median (DWP, 2003a).

Some types of people are more likely to be persistently poor than others (Jenkins and Rigg, 2001; DWP, 2003a). Those most at risk of persistent poverty (poor for at least three out of four consecutive years) are:

- children

- pensioners, especially pensioner couples

- lone parents

- social housing tenants

- adults with no educational qualifications

- people in workless households.

Poverty exit and entry rates

The fact that some types of people are more likely to remain poor than others means that the rate at which they escape from poverty is lower than it is for those who are less likely to be persistently poor. Table 3 shows the rate at which people exited or entered poverty during the 1990s (1991 to 1999) in Britain (see Jenkins and Rigg, 2001). For comparison, it also shows the risk of poverty (the percentage of individuals in each household type who were poor) averaged over this period.

The poverty *exit rate* is computed as the number of people who left poverty between one year and the next as a percentage of the total number of poor households. The poverty *entry rate* is

11

Table 3 Poverty risk, exit rate and entry rate, 1991–99 (per cent of individuals)

	Risk	Exit rate	Entry rate
Pensioner couple	22	32	9
Single pensioner	34	30	15
Couple with children	18	36	8
Couple with children and other adults	14	58	8
Couple without children	8	50	4
Lone parent	49	28	24
Single	20	43	8
All individuals	19	37	8

See definitions of poverty risk, exit and entry rates in the text.

Source: Jenkins and Rigg (2001, Table 3.1).

the number of people who entered poverty between one year and the next as a percentage of the number of people who were non-poor (Jenkins and Rigg, 2001). *It is important to note that the poverty exit rate tends to be higher than the entry rate because it is calculated on a smaller number of people* (fewer people are poor than are non-poor).

In the 1990s, 37 per cent of poor people escaped from poverty between one year and the next. In other words, every year, on average, over one in three people experiencing poverty became non-poor (though, as we noted above, in most cases they did not move very far up the income scale). Meanwhile, 8 per cent of non-poor people became poor each year on average during the 1990s (Table 3).

The poverty exit rate was especially high for individuals living in households containing couples without children and couples with children where other adults were living in the household. On average, half of poor individuals living in such households escaped from poverty each year. Yet these were the people who were the least likely to be poor in the first place. Thus, on average, only 8 per cent of childless couples were poor in Britain during the 1990s. The poverty entry rate was correspondingly low at only 4 per cent (Table 3).

The poverty exit rate was lowest for individuals living in lone-parent and in pensioner households. The chance of someone living in a lone-parent household escaping from poverty each year was only 28 per cent. For single pensioners, the poverty exit rate was 30 per cent and, for individuals living in pensioner couple households, it was 32 per cent (Table 3).

Poverty entry rates were very high for individuals living in lone-parent households. At 24 per cent, the poverty entry rate for these people was three times the national average. In other words, every year on average, a quarter of lone parents became poor. Single pensioners had a poverty entry rate that was double the average for the population as a whole during the 1990s (Table 3).

Routes out of poverty

Recent research has begun to examine the events that are associated with or 'trigger' exits from, and entries into, income poverty (Jarvis and Jenkins, 1997; Jenkins, 2000; Jenkins and Rigg, 2001). The focus here is on events associated with exits from poverty.

Routes out of poverty can involve changes in household income, changes in the size or composition of households, or both simultaneously. *Income events* that might trigger moves out of poverty include moves from benefit into work and rises in take-home pay. *Demographic events* include changes such as lone parents repartnering or children leaving home. In addition, *health events* can trigger exits out of poverty. For example, improvement in mental health can make it possible for people of working age to move back into work.

Jenkins and Rigg (2001) examined events triggering moves out of poverty (defined as incomes below 60 per cent of median income before housing costs) during the nine years from 1991 to 1999. When poverty exits were classified into mutually exclusive categories according to the *main* trigger event, income changes were the most important. Altogether, four out of five exits from poverty by individuals were triggered by income events and only one in five by demographic events. Some three-quarters of the *income* events were associated with paid work. In total, 33 per cent of *all* poverty exits were triggered by a rise in the head of household's earnings from paid work; a further 17 per cent were triggered by a rise in spouse's labour earnings; and 12 per cent by other labour earnings (Jenkins and Rigg, 2001).

Some exit routes are more relevant to certain types of household than others. For example, for people of working age, events associated with the labour market are more relevant than they are for people over state retirement age. Table 4 shows the importance of different types of *main* event associated with exits out of poverty for different types of household. As might be expected, changes in non-labour income such as pensions were by far the most important type of event associated with exits out of poverty for pensioners, especially single pensioners. For people of working age, an increase in labour earnings – either for the head of household or partner – was the main event associated with an exit from poverty. However, as Jenkins and Rigg (2001) point out, what is especially noticeable from Table 4 is the relative importance of labour market events involving adults other than the household head. Second-earners can make an important difference in helping households to escape from poverty.

The data in Table 4 refers to mutually exclusive 'main events' associated with poverty exits. However, in practice, events often happen in conjunction with others rather than on their own. For example, repartnering may provide the opportunity for a lone parent to take up a part-time job.

14

Table 4 Poverty exits and trigger events, by person's household type in last year of poverty spell (percentages)

Main event associated with poverty exit	All	Single pensioner	Pensioner couple	Single	Couple no children	Couple and children	Lone parent	Other
Household head's labour earnings rose	33	5	2	40	32	41	38	9
Spouse's or other labour earnings rose	29	3	14	9	28	35	34	35
Non-labour income rose	20	87	65	20	22	7	15	17
Demographic event	19	6	20	31	18	17	14	39
All poverty exits	100	100	100	100	100	100	100	100

Columns may not sum to 100 because of rounding errors.

Source: Jenkins and Rigg (2001, Table 3.3).

As well as the *main* event, poverty exits can also be classified according to *all* events associated with an exit (Jenkins and Rigg, 2001). This produces a list that is not mutually exclusive – as an exit can be associated with more than one event – and that consequently will tend to sum to more than 100 per cent. Table 5 shows the importance of various types of event in relation to the prevalence of the event, the extent to which it was associated with exit from poverty and the share of all exits that it accounted for. The share of poverty exits associated with an event is related to both its prevalence and the extent to which it tends to lift people out of poverty. For instance, a high proportion of people experiencing a particular event may escape from poverty, but, if the incidence of that event is very low, the total number of people affected will be small (Jenkins and Rigg, 2001). Thus, while 79 per cent of individuals in households of unchanged size that had a rise in benefit income exited poverty, only 6 per cent of people experienced the event. The net result was that this type of event accounted for just 12 per cent of exits from poverty (Table 5).

Table 5 shows that there is a 'diversity of routes out of poverty' (Jenkins and Rigg, 2001, p. 50). However, some routes are more important than others. Labour market events are still the most common route out of poverty. An increase in the number of workers in a household with an unchanged size accounted for the largest share of exits out of poverty. A rise in the number of full-time workers and a rise in labour market earnings were also important triggers for poverty exits. A rise in non-labour, non-benefit income was associated with about a fifth of all exits from poverty. Meanwhile, changes in household type and falls in the number of people with poor mental health each accounted for about one in six poverty exits (Table 5). Not surprisingly, the importance of different types of event varied between the different types of household.

Table 5 Trigger events and exits from poverty among all persons in poor households

Event type	Prevalence of event	Cell percentages	
		Exit rate associated with event	Share of all exits associated with event
Exit rate among all persons in poor households = 37%			
Labour market events			
Rise in labour earnings (same number of workers)	13	58	20
Rise in number of workers (same household size)	16	64	28
Rise in number of full-time workers (same household size)	11	70	20
Non-labour income events			
Rise in benefit income (same household size)	6	79	12
Rise in non-benefit, non-labour income (same household size)	11	65	19
Demographic events			
Change in household type	12	51	17
Moved to married couple household	2	64	3
Health events			
Fall in number with poor mental health (same household size)	16	39	17
Fall in number with daily activities limited by health (same household size)	11	37	11

Events are not mutually exclusive.
Source: Jenkins and Rigg (2001, Table 3.6).

For individuals in *lone-parent* households, labour market events were less important, and demographic events more important, than they were for the population as a whole (Jenkins and Rigg, 2001). The events associated with the largest share of exits were:

- rise in the number of workers (same household size) – 28 per cent of exits

- change in household type – 26 per cent of exits

- move to couple household – 18 per cent of exits

- move to couple household and rise in number of workers – 17 per cent of exits

- rise in non-benefit, non-labour income (same household size) – 17 per cent of exits.

For lone parents, the event most likely to be associated with escape from poverty was moving into a couple household and rise in the number of workers. Indeed, 92 per cent of lone parents experiencing this joint event escaped from poverty. However, since it affected only 5 per cent of lone parents, it accounted for only 17 per cent of lone-parent poverty exits. It is clear that repartnering, where it is accompanied by a move into paid work, is a highly effective route out of poverty.

For individuals in *couples with children*, the events most commonly associated with escape from poverty were:

- rise in number of workers (same household size) – 40 per cent of exits

- rise in labour earnings (same number of workers) – 31 per cent of exits

- rise in number of full-time workers – 30 per cent of exits

- fall in number with poor mental health (same household size) – 21 per cent of exits.

For couples with children, labour market events were the most common ladder out of poverty (Jenkins and Rigg, 2001). The relatively high prevalence of events such as a rise in labour earnings or in the number of workers in the household, combined with the high proportion of them that resulted in an exit from poverty, ensured that they accounted for a high proportion of poverty exits among couples with children. Demographic events, such as changes in household type or reductions in the number of children in the household, were much less important.

For individuals in *pensioner* households, labour market events (not surprisingly) and demographic events were not very important. Instead, increases in non-benefit, non-labour income were the most common route out of poverty:

> This event accounted for almost one-third (30 per cent) of poverty exits by single pensioners and almost half (48 per cent) of exits by pensioner couples. No other event came close in terms of aggregate importance.
>
> (Jenkins and Rigg, 2001, p. 54)

This income source comprised mainly private and occupational pensions as well as savings. The next most common route out of poverty was improvements in mental and physical health, mainly because they had a relatively high incidence among the elderly.

19

Although very few pensioners were affected by labour market events, where they did occur, they were associated with a very high poverty exit rate. For example, among pensioner couples, 82 per cent of those who were in households that experienced an increase in the number of workers (same household size) escaped from poverty. Among those who experienced a rise in labour market earnings (same household size), the poverty exit rate was 79 per cent (Jenkins and Rigg, 2001). This implies that work could be an effective route out of poverty for the minority of people over pensionable age who are both able and wish to work. That in turn suggests that tackling age discrimination in the workplace could act as a modestly important ladder out of poverty for some older people.

Rises in benefit income (same household size) were also very effective in lifting pensioners out of poverty but very few experienced this event. The poverty exit rate among those affected by such an event was 87 per cent in the case of single poor pensioners and 92 per cent in the case of individuals in couple pensioner households. This suggests that 'if the Minimum Income Guarantee can be made to work (with a high take-up rate), there will be a marked reduction in low income among pensioners' (Jenkins and Rigg, 2001, p. 56).[4]

Poverty trajectories

We have seen that, although there is income mobility, most people in poverty do not escape very far, if at all; and some of those who do escape return after a short period. For instance, Walker (1998b) found one in five Income Support (Jobseeker's Allowance) claimants could expect to be back on benefit within six months. Shorter periods on Income Support were more likely than longer periods to lead to a recurrence on benefit (Shaw *et al.*, 1996).

There is in fact a diverse range of 'poverty trajectories' over time (Ashworth et al., 1994; Walker and Ashworth, 1994). Gardiner and Hills (1999) – drawing on work by Jarvis and Jenkins (1997) – analysed the income trajectories of respondents who were interviewed in all four waves of the British Household Panel Survey (BHPS) between 1991 and 1994. They identified five basic income trajectories:

1   flat

2   rising

3   falling

4   blips

5   other.

Gardiner and Hills (1999) defined flat trajectories as occurring where people remained within the same income group or its near neighbour throughout the four-year period. Rising and falling income trajectories occurred where people moved significantly upwards or downwards respectively across the period. Those starting or ending up in the bottom income group were defined as rising out of, or falling into, poverty respectively. Blips were broadly flat income trajectories, but with one period in poverty (blip into poverty) or one period out of poverty (blip out of poverty), before returning to the original position. Finally, other trajectories covered all others including those that represented repeated poverty (two or more years in poverty) and one-off poverty (one year in the bottom two income groups).

Table 6 Poverty trajectories

Trajectory type	%
Flat	40.5
Rising out of poverty	5.4
Falling into poverty	3.6
Blips – out of poverty	20.6
Blips – into poverty	7.1
Other – repeated poverty	13.7
Other – one-off poverty	7.5

Note: based on the first four waves of the BHPS.

Source: Gardiner and Hills (1999, Table 6).

Table 6 shows, for people who were poor at any one of the four BHPS interviews from 1991 to 1994, the percentage that experienced one or other of these trajectories. Most people affected by poverty had a flat trajectory (41 per cent), that is, they were poor throughout the four-year period. The next most common trajectory was a blip, either into or out of poverty (28 per cent). Meanwhile, 14 per cent experienced repeated poverty. Relatively few cases involved simply rising out of or falling into poverty (9 per cent). Thus, it is clear that there is a complex set of poverty trajectories, but the policy implications are likely to differ according to different trajectories (Gardiner and Hills, 1999).

Key points

The key points to emerge from this chapter are as follows.

- There is considerable income mobility from one year to the next and, consequently, movement among individuals into and out of poverty.

- Although there is much movement, it tends to be quite short range: most people do not move very far up or down the income distribution.

- A minority of people are persistently poor. Those most at risk of being persistently poor are children, lone parents and pensioners.

- For people of working age, labour market events are much more important triggers for poverty exits than household demographic events or health events. For pensioners, changes in non-labour income such as pensions are more important.

- There is a complex set of poverty trajectories, but the implications for poverty differ according to the different trajectories.

3   Work as a ladder out of poverty

The Labour Government has argued that work is the surest and best route out of poverty. The evidence presented in the previous chapter certainly showed that moving into paid work was the event most commonly associated with exits from poverty among people of working age. In this chapter, we therefore examine this important ladder in more depth.

Worklessness and poverty

Table 7 shows the incidence or risk of poverty among adults of working age in Britain and is drawn from the most recent report of *Households Below Average Income*. It clearly indicates an association between worklessness and poverty. Almost half (47 per cent) of working-age adults living in workless households are poor, that is, have a disposable income after housing costs that is less than 60 per cent of the median. By contrast, among adults living in households where at least one person is in paid work, only 9 per cent of adults are poor. Expressed differently, the risk of poverty is five times greater among adults in workless households than among those in working households.

The risk of poverty is lowest among single people working full time and couples where both are working. Although still below the average for all adults as a whole, the risk of poverty is much higher where only one partner is working than where both are in paid work (irrespective of whether the 'second-earner' works full

24

Table 7 Risk and composition of low income* among working-age adults 2001/02

	Risk of low income (%)	Composition of low income (%)
Economic status of adults in the family		
One or more full-time self-employed	17	12
Single/couple all in full-time work	2	5
Couple, one full-time, one part-time	3	3
Couple, one full-time, one not working	11	9
No full-time, one or more part-time work	24	15
Workless, head or spouse aged 60 or over	34	7
Workless, head or spouse unemployed	60	14
Workless, other inactive	39	34
All adults	14	100
Economic status of household		
Households with one or more workers	9	54
Workless households	47	46
All adults	14	100

* Below 60 per cent of median income before housing costs.

Source: DWP (2003a, Tables 5.4 and 5.7).

or part time). It is increasingly necessary for both partners to be working in order for a couple to keep out of poverty (Gregg and Wadsworth, 1996).

The risk of poverty among *workless* households of working age varies according to the economic status of the head of household or spouse (Table 7). It is much higher among working-age adults in households where the head or spouse is unemployed (60 per cent) than when they are either aged over 60 years (34 per cent) or inactive (39 per cent). In this context, 'inactive' means families in which all the adults are neither in work nor unemployed. These economically inactive adults of working age are mainly lone parents and people in receipt of sickness and disability benefits. They are the largest single group of working-age adults living in poverty. They account for a third (34 per cent) of all poor adults but only 12 per cent of the total population of working-age adults. Lone parents and disabled people are not required to engage in job search in return for receiving social security benefits, but – apart from the more severely disabled – they are now obliged to attend work-focused interviews with Jobcentre Plus personal advisers.

Whereas the poverty rate for people in full-time paid employment is below the average for all households, among people in full-time self-employment, it is above average. This suggests that self-employment may be a less sure ladder out of poverty than employment, at least for some people.

Table 8 shows labour market events associated with exits from poverty among lone parents and couples with children in Britain during the period from 1991 to 1999 (Jenkins and Rigg, 2001). For both types of household, the event that accounted for the largest share of exits from poverty was a rise in the number of workers (same household size). This confirms that paid employment is an important ladder out of poverty.

However, only about half (53 per cent) of lone parents that experienced a rise in the number of workers in the household actually moved out of poverty. Among couples with children, three-fifths (62 per cent) did so. In other words, in the 1990s, a very substantial minority of poor people in families with children that had a rise in the number of workers nonetheless remained in poverty. About two-thirds of people living in families with children where there was a rise in labour market earnings escaped from poverty, but about a third remained poor (Table 8).

Thus, although paid work is the most common route out of poverty, it is not a guaranteed one. Just over half (54 per cent) of poor adults of working age live in households where at least one person is working (Table 7). Or, to put it another way, 2.6 million working-age adults living in households where at least one person is in work are poor.

Table 8 Labour market events and exits from poverty among poor families with children (on percentages)

	Prevalence of event	Exit rate associated with event	Share of all exits associated with event
Lone parents			
Rise in labour earnings (number of workers the same)	8	49	13
Rise in number of workers (same household size)	15	53	28
Rise in number of full-time workers (same household size)	5	66	11
Move to couple household and rise in number of workers	5	92	17
Couples with children			
Rise in labour earnings (number of workers the same)	21	53	31
Rise in number of workers (same household size)	23	62	40
Rise in number of full-time workers (same household size)	17	65	30

Source: Jenkins and Rigg (2001, Tables 3.7 and 3.8).

Low pay

One reason why work is not always a route out of poverty is that some jobs are low paid. Webb *et al.* (1996) estimated that about a fifth of the workforce was low paid (defined as two-thirds of median hourly wages). They found an important gender dimension to low pay: about two-thirds of low-paid employees were women and around one in three female workers were on low pay. The majority of low-paid employees were young single people or married and cohabiting women (Webb *et al.*, 1996).

Low pay is concentrated among certain industries (such as catering, retail and residential care) and occupations (like hairdressing, cleaners and security guards). As well as women and young people, the types of individuals most likely to be low paid include:

- employees working part time

- people from minority ethnic groups

- long-term sick and disabled people

- older male workers

- people with low levels of qualifications or none at all

- people with little or no work experience (Sloane and Theodossiou, 1996; McKnight, 2002).

The incidence of low pay has increased substantially over the past quarter of a century. The percentage of employees earning less than two-thirds of the median employee increased from 12 per cent in 1977 to 21 per cent in 1998. The increased incidence

28

of low pay has been part of a sharp increase in earnings inequality. The earnings of the well paid have increased much more than those of the poorest paid employees (McKnight, 2002).

The reasons for the increase in earnings inequality are not fully clear. Part of the explanation is believed to be a fall in the demand for unskilled labour as a result of changes in technology and trade patterns (Nickell, 1996). At the same time, there has been an increase in the wage premium obtained by people with high qualifications compared to those with low education or skills (HM Treasury and DWP, 2001). It is possible that this wage premium may decline as an increasing number of young people go into higher education, but it is likely to remain important for the foreseeable future. Wage inequality among male workers with low levels of education and skills has also increased. This suggests that the marked rise in earnings inequality since the 1970s cannot be attributed solely to changes in the demand for skills (Nickell, 1996).

The existence of low-paid jobs may be less of a problem where there is earnings mobility than where there is immobility. In other words, we might be less concerned about people being low paid if there is scope for them to move into better-paid employment in due course. But, in fact, most income mobility is over quite a short range and there is considerable earnings immobility (Machin, 1998; Dickens, 1999). Moreover, earnings mobility appears to have fallen since the late 1970s (Dickens, 1999). This implies that it is now more difficult for people to move out of low pay over time. Thus, not only has wage inequality increased, but the low paid are much less likely to escape from low pay:

> Given that we have also seen a sharp rise in ... wage inequality over this time period, this tells us that not only has the gap between rich and poor risen but the ability of

29

> the low paid to close this gap has fallen considerably. Far from offsetting the increase in ... wage inequality, changes in mobility appear to have exacerbated this rise.
>
> (Dickens, 1998, p. 80)

Other evidence confirms that there is a strong degree of persistence in low pay from one year to the next. Low pay is not a transient experience for many low-paid employees: low-paid workers tend to remain low paid. The persistence of low pay is related not only to the characteristics of the workers concerned, but also to the very fact of having been low paid. In other words, being low paid in one period 'in itself increases the probability of being low paid in the next period' (Stewart and Swaffield, 1999). The net result is that low-paid jobs do not act as stepping stones to better-paid jobs; they are more likely to constitute blind alleys from which there is relatively little prospect of escape (Stewart, 1999).

Low-paid jobs also tend to be more precarious than higher-paid jobs (McKnight, 2002). The people who are low paid are more likely than those who are better paid to become unemployed in the next year. They are also more likely to be low paid when they return to work (Stewart, 1999). Indeed, there appears to be a 'low-pay, no-pay' cycle in which periods of low pay are interspersed with periods of unemployment (Dickens, 1999; Stewart, 1999; Stewart and Swaffield, 1999). In this context, policies to facilitate job retention could play an important role (Kellard, 2002).

Unemployment appears to have a negative impact – or 'scarring effect' – on future earnings, thereby helping to perpetuate low pay. Moreover, this wage penalty increases with length of time out of work. One study found that, on average, unemployed people taking up a job after an involuntary job loss earned 9 per cent less than in their previous job. When compared with workers in continuous employment, the average wage loss of someone returning to work after an involuntary job loss was 14 per cent (Gregg, 1998). Another study concluded that:

> Joblessness leaves permanent scars on individuals. They not only lose income during periods of joblessness they are also further scarred by the experience when they find employment. A spell of unemployment is found to carry a wage penalty of about six per cent on re-entry in Britain and after three years they are earning 14 per cent less compared with what they would have received in the absence of unemployment.
>
> (Arulampalam, 2001, p. F585)

Research by Gregg and Wadsworth (2000) shows that the wages of jobs taken by people who are out of work – 'entry jobs' – are substantially below the average for other jobs. They found that the median weekly earnings of entry jobs in 1997/98 was only half that of all jobs and two-thirds that of jobs taken by people moving from one job to another. Entry jobs were much less likely to be full-time and permanent than other jobs. It was also found that the gap between the wages of entry jobs and other jobs had increased rapidly since 1979. In real terms, entry job wages stagnated over this period while the wages of other jobs rose (Gregg and Wadsworth, 2000). However, since 1997, adult entry wages have risen more than the wages of jobs in general, probably in response to the tighter labour market that has developed with the sustained fall in unemployment (Gregg and Pasanen, 2001).

Low pay and household poverty

The low paid are not necessarily poor. Whether they are poor depends partly on, not just their rate of pay, but also how many

31

hours they work, including whether they do overtime and how many jobs they have. Some people may be able to offset low pay by working very long hours or having more than one job. It also depends on whether they are claiming in-work benefits or tax credits and, if so, the amount received. And it also depends on the income, if any, received by other people in the household. This reflects the fact that low pay refers to individuals, whereas poverty is usually measured on a household income basis (McKnight, 2002).

Research by Dickens (cited by McKnight, 2002) indicates that the proportion of poor people who are working has increased, rising from 4 per cent in 1968 to 10 per cent in 1996. In other words, employment became a slightly less sure ladder out of poverty over this period. The poverty rate among working households is particularly high where there is only one worker and that person is low paid. Between 1968 and 1996, the proportion of one-earner households living in poverty doubled, rising from a quarter to one half. Meanwhile, the proportion of the population in employment over the same time period fell from 70 to 55 per cent (McKnight, 2002).

Webb *et al.* (1996) found that the proportion of low-paid employees living in household poverty has increased, rising from 3 to 4 per cent at the end of the 1960s to 13 per cent in the mid-1990s. They also examined what was keeping low-paid employees above the poverty line (defined as 50 per cent of mean disposable income before housing costs). The results showed that very few low-paid employees were able to avoid poverty just through their own market income (Table 9). Those who did were mainly single people with no dependants and those who worked long hours. The two main factors lifting low-paid people out of poverty were their partner's income and income from other people in the household (such as non-dependent children).

Table 9 Escape routes from household poverty among low-paid employees

Means of escaping household poverty	% of low-paid employees
Own market income	8.2
Spouse's market income	40.8
Non-means-tested benefits	3.7
Means-tested benefits	4.5
Others' income	30.5
In poverty	12.4
Total	100

Source: Webb *et al.* (1996, Table 2).

Social security benefits played very little role in lifting the low paid out of poverty, irrespective of whether they were means tested or not (Webb *et al.*, 1996). The main in-work benefit available when Webb *et al.*'s research was undertaken was Family Credit. This benefit was replaced by the more generous Working Families' Tax Credit in October 1999, which was itself replaced by the Working Tax Credit and Child Tax Credit in April 2003. Because they are together more generous than Family Credit, these new tax credits should be having a greater impact in lifting the low paid out of poverty.

Another important development affecting the overlap between poverty and low pay is the national minimum wage (NMW), which was introduced in April 1999. It was initially set at £3.60 per hour and is now £4.50. There is a lower rate of £3.80 per hour for people aged 18 to 21 years. Dickens (2001) estimated that the NMW raised the pay of about 1.3 million workers or about 5 to 6 per cent of all employees. About three-quarters of those affected are women (Metcalf, 2002). The increase in wage inequality during the 1980s and 1990s means that there is now a stronger link between low pay and low household income. Consequently, the national minimum wage is a more effective tool for tackling poverty than it would have been two decades ago (Dickens, 2001; Metcalf, 2002).

Exclusion from paid work

Despite having one of the lowest unemployment rates among the OECD countries, Britain also has one of the highest rates of workless households. Currently, about one in six working-age households has no adult in paid employment. The great majority of adults in workless households are not actively seeking work. In 2000, less than one in five were doing so (Gregg and Wadsworth, 2001).

Berthoud (2003b) examined non-employment (defined as being either not working at least 16 hours a week or not in full-time education, *and* not having a working partner) in Britain between 1992 and 2000. He found that the people most at risk of experiencing non-employment were:

• men and women without a partner, especially lone parents

• disabled people

• people with low qualifications and skills

• people in their fifties

• people living in areas of weak labour demand

• members of certain minority ethnic groups.

The more of these disadvantages people had, the greater the risk of them being non-employed. About one in ten had at least three of them and very few indeed had all six (Berthoud, 2003b). These disadvantages are similar to the risk factors for being in low-paid employment. This suggests that, not only are people in these groups more likely to be without work, but also, if they are in work, they are more likely to be low paid (Bradshaw *et al.*, 2003).

Lakey *et al.*'s (2001) qualitative study of the employment difficulties of young people with multiple disadvantages focused on those with experience of homelessness, disability, poor mental health, drug and alcohol problems, poor literacy and language skills, having been in care, early motherhood and problems with the law. They found that these disadvantages made it difficult for the young people to obtain work and especially secure jobs. Most had spent their working lives moving in and out of jobs that were temporary, casual or part-time.

Since 1997, various New Deals have been introduced to improve employability and help the long-term unemployed and economically inactive people into work. The emerging evaluations of these programmes point to modest success in helping people into unsubsidised jobs (Nickell and Quintini, 2002). Even so, these programmes have been better able to help those who are the reasonably 'job ready' than people who are more detached from the labour market. Moreover, there are concerns that the New Deal is better at getting people into jobs than it is at helping them to stay in work. Job retention is therefore becoming an increasingly important issue for policy (Kellard, 2002).

For some economically inactive people, including the most severely disabled people, paid employment is not a realistic option and therefore not a ladder out of poverty. Most are reliant on social security benefits for their income. For such households, improvements in social security benefits are likely to be the most important route out of poverty (Gardiner and Hills, 1999).

Key points

The key points to emerge from this chapter are as follows.

- There is a close association between poverty and worklessness.

- Paid employment is an important ladder out of poverty.

- The incidence of low pay has increased in recent decades, thereby reducing the efficacy of work as a route out of poverty.

- There is evidence of a low-pay, no-pay cycle in which people move from unemployment into low-paid work and back again.

- Many low-paid earners live in non-poor households.

- Britain has low unemployment but high levels of economic inactivity.

- Some of the most severely disadvantaged people are a long way from the labour market and are hard to employ.

- For some economically inactive people, especially the most severely disabled, paid employment is not a realistic option. In these cases, increases in social security benefit levels could be the most important ladder out of poverty.

4   YOUNG PEOPLE

Youth can be defined as a period of semi-independence during which the transition from childhood to adulthood occurs (Jones and Wallace, 1992; G. Jones, 2002). In the last couple of decades, youth transitions have become more protracted and, in the case of the most disadvantaged, more fractured (Furlong and Cartmel, 1997).

The transition from childhood to adulthood has been described as taking place on three interconnected pathways: the school-to-work transition; the domestic transition; and the housing transition (Coles, 1995). The school-to-work transition describes the move from full-time education and training towards a full-time job in the labour market. The domestic transition comprises the progress from family of origin towards establishing a family of one's own. The housing transition is the process of moving out of residence with parents into independent living. These transitions can be described as 'careers' in the sense of sequences of varied experiences leading to different destinations (MacDonald *et al.*, 2001).

Youth poverty dynamics

In contrast to child poverty, and to a lesser extent pensioner poverty, there is a relative lack of data and research into the poverty dynamics of 16 to 25 year olds. The situation is complicated by the distinction within this age group – based on economic activity – between young people who are school attendees (featured in DfES statistics) and those who left the education system (represented in DWP labour market statistics). Statistics measuring household poverty follow this distinction and class the former group as children and the latter as adults.

The latest publication of *Households Below Average Income* (DWP, 2003a) reveals the following main findings about poverty and young working-age people in 2001/02.

- Across age bands, those living in households where the head was under 25 had the greatest risk of low income. Most families with children where the head is under 25 are lone-parent families.

- Forty-five per cent of families with children with a head under 25 were in the bottom quintile and 31 per cent in the second quintile of the income distribution.

Further analysis of the Family Resources Survey is needed to examine poverty among young people.

The dynamics and persistence of poverty for various age groups is difficult to measure reliably because, with each wave of a longitudinal survey, individuals will become older and might cross over to different age groups. Nevertheless, Jenkins and Rigg (2001) found that the poverty rate and persistence of poverty for 16 to 25 year olds is at, or even slightly below, the national average. Between 1991 and 1999, 5 per cent of young people aged 16 to 25 experienced persistent poverty compared to 16 per cent of nought to four year olds and 20 per cent of people aged 75 and above (Jenkins and Rigg, 2001). In the same period, 59 per cent of young people never experienced poverty and 14 per cent experienced poverty as a one-off phenomenon.

Youth transitions

In the following sections, risk factors and protective factors of youth poverty are examined on the three pathways mentioned before: the school-to-work transition; the domestic transition; and the housing transition. Youth transitions are influenced by access to citizenship; state legislation and policy; interaction between young people, their families and professionals; localities; and individual 'agency' as young people make choices at 'critical points' (MacDonald *et al.*, 2001). Although some commentators argue that people have much more scope than in the past to shape their lives (Giddens, 1996), social and economic constraints remain important factors for many young people (Furlong and Cartmel, 1997). Structural constraints on career paths are imposed mainly by family relationships and by labour market and housing conditions, while agency stems from one's own character and social capital. Various studies (Coles, 1995; Hodkinson and Sparkes, 1997) have emphasised the importance of so-called 'critical moments' and life events as turning points in individual life careers. Changing family situations (death/divorce) and encounters with professionals (such as teachers, social workers and personal advisers) can significantly affect the life course of someone. Young people often explain their current situation by referring to these critical moments in their lives (MacDonald *et al.*, 2001).

The school-to-work transition

The interconnected factors of educational qualifications and employment status contribute significantly to the risk of entering poverty. This section reviews young people's main economic activities and the outcomes that might lead them into or out of poverty. The statistics presented here are based on two waves

39

of the Youth Cohort Study (YCS) (DfES, 2001, 2003a, 2003b) carried out in 2000 and 2002. The YCS is the main source of survey information about the education, training and work experiences of young people in England and Wales, and it contains longitudinal data on youth transitions from education to employment. Table 10 describes the main economic activities of 16, 18 and 21 year olds in the UK in 2000/02.

Overall, participation in education was closely linked to activity at 16. Over a third of those in full-time education at 16 were in full-time education at 21, compared to only one in 20 of those who were employed, in government-supported training or 'not in employment, education or training' (NEET) at 16. Some 22 per cent of those who were NEET at 16 were looking after a home or family at 21. Those with no or low qualifications and those from unskilled manual backgrounds, almost all women, were most likely to look after the home and family (DfES, 2001).

Changes in the nature of the labour market and in social structures (e.g. less stable families) mean that young people face new risks and challenges when making the transition from education to employment (G. Jones, 2002). In today's labour market, there is a bigger demand for a highly trained workforce

Table 10 Young people's economic activities at ages 16/18/21, UK, 2000/02, percentages

	16 year olds[a]	18 year olds[a]	21 year olds[b]
Full-time education	71	40	26
Government-supported training	9	8	4
Full-time job	9	31	52
Part-time job	3	7	6
Looking after home	–	2	4
NEET[c]	7	13	9

a Youth Cohort Study, Spring 2002.
b Youth Cohort Study, Autumn 2000.
c Not in employment, education or training.

while traditional craft apprenticeship routes to employment have declined (Robinson, 1999). There is also less likelihood of gaining a 'job for life', which brings the prospect of periodic job change and 'lifelong learning' (Gregg and Wadsworth, 1999). Accordingly, most young people spend more time in learning and those who do not will have fewer opportunities and a more insecure outlook later on. Longer learning, on the other hand, entails longer dependence on parental support, hence delayed financial independence.

The earning power of those young people who opt out of the education system when reaching 16 years of age remains low and puts them at an increased risk of short- and long-term poverty. In 2003, those aged 21 to 24 earned twice as much as under-18s. The average hourly wage of a full-time worker under 18 was £4.06, the hourly wage of 18 to 20 year olds was £5.95, while those aged 21 to 24 earned on average £8.10 per hour (New Earnings Survey, 2003). In 2003, over 230,000 young people aged 18 to 24 claimed social security benefits in the UK, of which 30 per cent were claimants for six to 12 months and 5 per cent for 12 to 24 months (ONS, 2004). Despite the New Deal for Young People (see below), long-term unemployment among young people has not been eliminated, though it is at a much lower level than it was in 1997.

The school-to-work transition can be compounded by one's socio-economic characteristics. Young people from minority ethnic backgrounds experience two to three times higher unemployment rates than white youth regardless of educational attainment (ONS, 1998). Young men are at a higher risk of unemployment than young women. In 2003, the unemployment rate of men (not in education) aged 18 to 24 was 12 per cent as opposed to 9 per cent of women in the same age group (ONS, 2004).

The housing transition

Parental home

Living at home[1] often prevents young people from becoming poor. Research has shown that unemployed men are more likely to find employment if living at home than when living alone or cohabiting. Living at home with employed parents also leads to positive outcomes. Possible reasons for this are financial support, encouragement and help with job search (G. Jones, 2002). The parental home can provide a route out of youth poverty by softening the impact of unemployment and low-paid jobs. By eliminating the risk of experiencing persistent poverty, the home environment can provide young people with the opportunity to follow their chosen career paths. On the other hand, living in a low-income household, in a lone-parent family or with a step-parent, can accelerate the leaving-home process and result in low educational attainment, early partnership formation, teenage pregnancy and poor (independent) housing conditions.

Living at home, especially in rural areas, can act as a constraint on transitions out of youth poverty (Pavis *et al.*, 2000). Unemployed or financially disadvantaged rural youth may have little choice but to stay at home longer. Similarly, they may have to study or work locally – leading to a restricted choice of higher educational institutions and employment options – because they cannot afford independent housing.

Independent housing

The supply of affordable housing available to young people has fallen because of a decline of social housing (Anderson, 1999), constraints on access to privately rented housing (Rugg, 1999) and an owner-occupier sector characterised by price inflation (Ford, 1999). Consequently, young people who do seek independent housing often find the cost unsustainable, live in poor conditions and experience frequent mobility and even homelessness (Rugg and Burrows, 1999). A recent study by Ford *et al.* (2002) found that, although traditional housing aspirations among young people remained the same, there is a considerable delay in being able to enter owner-occupation. Among those living independently, there is considerable housing mobility, three-quarters experiencing two or more moves and almost a third experiencing four or more since leaving the family home (Ford *et al.*, 2002). They found that 17 per cent of youth living independently experienced a period of homelessness, 72 per cent of whom had to sleep rough as a consequence. Young people living in independent housing often lived in poor physical conditions and needed parental support (Ford *et al.*, 2002). Hence, independent/transitional housing puts the majority of young people at the risk of (at least temporary) poverty.

Homelessness

There are approximately 32,000 homeless 16 to 21 year olds in Britain. A fifth of 16 to 24 year olds experience homelessness at some time in their lives (Social Exclusion Unit, 2002b). Most young homeless people leave the parental home because of family disruption, conflicts with parents, especially step-parents, physical violence and deprivation. Up to half of single homeless youth have experienced being looked after (G. Jones, 2002). The odds of experiencing (repeated) homelessness are higher among frequent movers, young people who have been in care or have lived with a step-parent at age 14, those who self-identify as Black Caribbean and runaways under age 16 (Ford *et al.*, 2002).

Young runaways aged 16 to 17 are more likely to sleep in dangerous places, travel longer distances and have mental health, drug and alcohol problems (Social Exclusion Unit, 2002b). Research shows that the health of young people sleeping rough is extremely poor (Mental Health Foundation, 1996). Young homeless people expose themselves to danger, to hunger and to physical and sexual abuse (Pleace *et al.*, 2000; Palmer, 2001).

Local youth cultures

Local youth cultures – that is, the meanings, values, identities and practices shared by different groups of young people – can form snakes or ladders into poverty. In the same locality, there can be several gendered definitions of what it means to be young and belong to a social group in a certain area. These belief systems influence attitudes towards formal institutions, especially school, employment and criminal activity (MacDonald *et al.*, 2001). In a study by MacDonald *et al.* (2001), young people reported that the area in which they lived circumscribed their life chances.

The domestic transition

Family of origin

Strained family relations can form a snake into poverty by leading to truancy, antisocial behaviour and youth homelessness. Young people from lone-mother households are twice as likely to have been suspended or expelled from school as those from other family types, irrespective of household income, tenure and family interaction (Scott and Bergman, 2002).

For young people with a disability, family resources are crucial for a successful transfer to independent living. In a study by Hendey and Pascall (2002), most disabled young people with jobs and independent households named parents as central to their achievements.

Local authority care

Young people who have been 'looked after' are generally at a very high risk of poverty in adulthood. The outcomes of having experienced local authority care are the following (Utting, 1997):

- more than 75 per cent of care-leavers have no academic qualifications of any kind

- more than 50 per cent of young people leaving care after 16 years old are unemployed

- 17 per cent of young women leaving care are pregnant or already mothers

- 10 per cent of 16- to 17-year-old claimants of severe hardship payments have been in care

- 23 per cent of adult prisoners and 38 per cent of young prisoners have been in care

- 30 per cent of single young homeless people have been in care.

The reasons for entering care in the first place are 'family misfortunes', such as homelessness, long-term parental illness, hospital confinement, absence of parents, imprisonment of parents and 'illegitimacy'. Most children in care are from disadvantaged families that receive social security benefits, live in poor, overcrowded housing and are either large or are headed by a lone parent (Sinclair and Gibbs, 2002).

Caring

There are 20,000 to 50,000 carers in the UK aged under 18, half of whom are aged 11 to 15 (Social Exclusion Unit, 2002b). Young people with caring responsibilities often miss out on education, which can later lead to unemployment and social exclusion. Caring for a parent with persistent mental health problems can result in young people leaving the parental home prematurely. On the other hand, young carers acquire practical skills, and mature and become independent earlier than their contemporaries. Yet these benefits are easily outweighed by decreased educational, social and employment opportunities (Dearden and Becker, 2000).

Drug use

In England and Wales, half (i.e. more than a million) of all 16 to 19 year olds have tried drugs. Over 100,000 have tried opiates and some 700,000 have tried hallucinogens. About 400,000 16 to 24 year olds have tried cocaine (Social Exclusion Unit, 2002b). Problematic drug use perpetuates youth and adult poverty through crime, unemployment and homelessness. The number of young people aged 15 to 24 starting treatment for problem drug use has doubled since the early 1990s and was around 30,000 in 2001 (Palmer *et al.*, 2002). Problem drug usage is associated with physical and mental ill health as well as increased risk of suicide (Neale, 2002). Drug treatment (such as substitute prescribing, detoxification and rehabilitation programmes) can be effective in helping people out of dependency (Gossop *et al.*, 1998, 2001) and thereby provide an indirect ladder out of poverty.

Family formation

Young people, especially men, who experience persistent poverty leave the parental home earlier than those who do not (Ermisch *et al.*, 2001). Early partnership formation (before the age of 19) increases the risk of early childbearing and single parenthood. Bynner *et al.* (2002) found that, of those young women who had formed early partnerships, 15 per cent were lone mothers by the age of 26. In 1999, 12 per cent of all lone-parent households were headed by an under 25 year old, over 90 per cent of whom were mothers (Millar and Ridge, 2001).

Teenage pregnancy

Teenage pregnancy is known to be associated with intergenerational poverty transfer. Living in a workless household between the ages of 11 to 15 substantially increases the chances of early childbearing for girls (Ermisch *et al.*, 2001). A study by Hobcraft and Kiernan (1999), based on the National Child Development Study, confirms these findings: 8 per cent of girls who did not experience childhood poverty became teenage mothers compared to 31 per cent who were assessed as poor.

Becoming a teenage mother is associated with high poverty risks. Early motherhood is more likely to precipitate an entry into social housing and to limit employment opportunities. Early mothers are more likely to be in receipt of non-universal benefits, and to have a low household income and no telephone at age 33. They are also more likely to smoke and to have poorer physical and mental health in adulthood (Hobcraft and Kiernan, 1999).

On the other hand, early parenthood can act as a potential ladder out of poverty for some young people. Teenage parents have access to benefits and social housing not available to all of their peers. Becoming a parent and caring for others is also associated with perceptions of maturity. Young people, especially women, report finding it easier to desist crime and have more motivation to find legal employment (Powers, 1996; Tabberer *et al.*, 2000; G. Jones, 2002) when they have a partner and a child.

Government support to young people

Government policy can act as ladders out of poverty. The Government is trying to tackle the skill deficit and unemployment among young people by various policies, including Modern Apprenticeships, the Right to Time off for Study and New Deal for Young People (NDYP) (G. Jones, 2002). Sixteen year olds are encouraged to remain in the education system by the means-tested Educational Maintenance Allowance and Youth Cards. Concerns about young people who are NEET have led to the development of the Connexions Strategy. The following sections briefly review the nature and impact of the main government policies targeting youth social exclusion.

Connexions

Connexions is a universal programme (implemented by the Connexions Service National Unit within the Department for Education and Skills), replacing the former Careers Service, which provides advice, guidance and support for 13 to 19 year olds, with the particular aim to encourage (re)connection with learning. Connexion is delivered through local partnerships (covering the same areas as Learning Skills Councils) and offers differentiated support to young people from various backgrounds with the help of Personal Advisers. The first pilots were introduced in April 2000 and, by March 2003, Connexions covered all of England. The various targets of the programme include education, care, drugs, offending and teenage pregnancy. The Treasury will judge the effectiveness of Connexions at the next and subsequent spending reviews on the basis of whether the proportion of young people who are NEET has declined. The target is to achieve a reduction in the proportion of young people who are NEET by 10 per cent by 2004 (Popham, 2003).

Education Maintenance Allowance

The Education Maintenance Allowance (EMA) is a government pilot scheme that started in September 1999 and ran for three years. Its purpose is to raise participation, retention and achievement in post-compulsory education among 16 to 18 year olds. It provides a means-tested allowance of up to £40 per week to young people in further education. The EMA is currently available across 56 local education authorities but it will be introduced on a national basis from September 2004. The main findings of EMA evaluation research (Maguire and Maguire, 2003) are:

- 6 per cent gain in participation in year 12 by eligible young people in the pilot areas compared to control areas

- 7.3 per cent gain in participation in year 13 by eligible young people in the pilot areas compared to control areas, mostly because of retention

- EMA had a significantly greater impact on young men, which may address the gender gap in performance of pupils in further education

- EMA had a positive impact on school attendance and effort on coursework

- EMA payment to the young person is more effective than payment to the parent

- higher bonuses per term improve retention.

In September 2000, four existing EMA pilot areas introduced a more flexible support (called EMA Vulnerable Pilot) and Childcare Pilots to meet the needs of more disadvantaged groups, namely, young people with disabilities, the homeless and teenage parents. The evaluation of these pilots found that students with disabilities tended to have more stable education trajectories and more settled domestic circumstances (Allen *et al.*, 2003). Young homeless people and teenage parents described financial barriers as key obstacles to return to education. Participation in EMA Vulnerable Pilots and Childcare Pilots had, not only financial and educational benefits for these young people, but also wider personal effects, improving self-esteem, levels of confidence, social interaction, independence and basic life skills such as financial management. In the implementation of EMA, the role of Personal Adviser is key (Allen *et al.*, 2003).

New Deal for Young People

New Deal for Young People (NDYP) was introduced throughout Great Britain in 1998 as a key element of the Government's welfare-to-work strategy. The NDYP is mandatory for young people aged 18 to 24 who have been unemployed for six months or longer. It has three components: Gateway, Options and Follow-through. During Gateway, the young person receives careers guidance from a Personal Adviser. At the end of this period, there are four placement options: six months' subsidised employment; six months' placement with a voluntary organisation; six months on an environmental task force; or up to 12 months' training towards an NVQ level 1 or 2. The Follow-through period is very similar to the Gateway and has the function of ensuring that New Deal participants continue with their job search or sustain their employment.

Since NDYP's launch in 1998, 955,300 young people have started it. Of these, 864,400 (90 per cent) have left, leaving 90,900 participants at the end of March 2003 (DWP, 2003b). Altogether, 39 per cent of all NDYP leavers entered sustained – that is, lasting longer than 13 weeks and young person does not return to New Deal – unsubsidised jobs, 12 per cent transferred to other benefits, 20 per cent left for other known reasons and 29 per cent left for unknown reasons.

Figure 1 describes the position (in March 2003) of those young people who had their first New Deal (for young people aged 18 to 24) interview in January 2002 and are presently not New Deal clients. Overall, most long-term leavers are in unsubsidised jobs or in unknown destinations. Those with an educational attainment of NVQ level 2 or higher had the biggest success rate (44 per cent) in finding unsubsidised employment. More men (35 per cent) and white youth (35 per cent) are in unsubsidised jobs than women (33 per cent) and minority ethnic youth (29 per cent). Women and people with disabilities are the main groups to transfer to other benefits. Ethnic minorities and people with no or below level 2 qualifications were more likely to leave to unknown destinations.

In an evaluation of the NDYP for minority ethnic youth (Fieldhouse *et al.*, 2002), young people reported the greatest satisfaction with the options of subsidised employment and full-time education. The NDYP's biggest achievements were quoted

Figure 1 March 2003 position of those NDYP leavers who had their first interview in January 2002 (percentages)

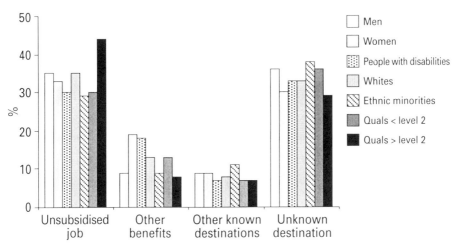

Source: DWP (2003b).

as enhancing employability, confidence and job-specific skills. Those young people who managed to secure employment were likely to have started out with a positive attitude towards work and also possessed the necessary social and cultural capital. The most commonly reported reasons for leaving NDYP are domestic responsibilities, deliberate avoidance because of disaffection, or finding alternative employment (Kalra *et al.*, 2001).

Gaps in the provision for young people

In spite of the Government's efforts to keep young people economically active (either through education or employment), policies are characterised by selectively targeting certain groups of young people while ignoring others. The national minimum wage, for example, disregards under-18 workers and provides reduced wages to 18 to 21 year olds compared to those aged over 22. Similarly, the New Deal for Young People denies support to 16- to 17-year-old school leavers, with the implicit understanding that they should be in further education. This is clearly not always the case. Meanwhile, 16 to 18 year olds have no access to Income Support and restricted access to other means-tested benefits. Housing Benefit for single people under 25 years renting privately is currently restricted to the average cost of shared (rather than self-contained) accommodation in the locality (Kemp and Rugg, 1996).

Those young people who choose to remain in education for longer are also at risk of experiencing poverty, especially debt. The replacement of student grants by loans and the abolition of student entitlement to Housing Benefit has had a considerable impact on student finances. Callender and Kemp (2000) found that 87 per cent of full-time students reported experiencing some financial difficulties and lone-parent students were the most vulnerable group to poverty. On the other hand, the substantial expansion of university places has increased the opportunity for young people from low-income backgrounds to go to university.

Key points

The key points to emerge from this chapter are as follows.

- By comparison with child and pensioner poverty, there has been relatively little statistical analysis of youth poverty.

- Youth is a period of transition from childhood to adulthood, which has become more protracted and, for some, more fractured than in the past. Critical points in this transition can act as ladders out of poverty or as snakes into poverty.

- Success in education and training is an increasingly important route to well-paid and more secure jobs. With the decline of the traditional craft apprenticeships, the labour market opportunities for those young people who gain little or no educational qualifications are often low paid and insecure. There is evidence of increasing polarisation between those who stay on in education or training and gain qualifications and those who do not.

- The family can act as an important protective factor in preventing young people falling into poverty, but, for a minority of young people, it can be more of a snake than a ladder.

- The New Deal for Young People has made an important difference in helping young people into work but those who are hardest to help have benefited much less.

5 FAMILIES WITH CHILDREN

There is evidence that child poverty is linked to negative outcomes in the long term and that many of the long-term outcomes bring with them hardship. Thus, disadvantage is transmitted across generations (Gregg *et al.*, 1999) and poverty itself is a snake. But childhood is also an important life stage in its own right, and child poverty affects the quality of life and well-being of children themselves. Child poverty is damaging both in the short and the long term.

But not all poor children experience the negative aspects of poverty, and poverty in childhood does not by definition mean that poverty and disadvantage will persist into adulthood. This suggests that children can be shielded from the negative effects of poverty. Creating a ladder out of poverty for children is an investment against both present and future poverty, and therefore facilitates the economic development of the nation. Because children are vulnerable and depend on others to look after and raise them, we also have a moral incentive to provide a ladder out of poverty for them.

Child poverty

Much of the evidence on child poverty has focused on a snapshot approach. This kind of analysis is important in that it gives us information about the characteristics of children living in poverty, which can inform the kinds of ladders needed to enable adults to lift children out of poverty. The latest *HBAI* 2001/02 statistics show that children generally are vulnerable to poverty relative to the rest of the population; they are more likely to be in the bottom two quintiles of the income distribution and less likely to be in the top two quintiles than the population as a whole. Box 1 shows the characteristics of poor children.

Box 1 Characteristics of poor children
Children have a higher risk of income poverty if they live in:

- lone-parent families
- workless families
- large families – three or more children (the risk increases with each extra child)
- families containing one or more disabled persons
- households headed by an ethnic minority, especially Pakistani or Bangladeshi origin
- families where the youngest child is aged under five
- families where the mother of the family is aged under 25
- households claiming benefit, especially Income Support or Housing Benefit
- inner London (after housing costs)
- rented accommodation, especially social rented accommodation
- families with no savings or assets.

Source: DWP (2002a).

Many poor children belong to two or more of these groups, leading to greater hardship. For example, the risk of poverty for children in the families headed by someone who is an ethnic minority is heightened by the risk of poverty for children in large families (HM Treasury, 1999b). Taking this into account, ladders out of poverty need to be multi-faceted to work.

A significant minority of children experience long-term poverty – 5 per cent of children in Britain have been on the bottom rung of the ladder for five consecutive years. Indeed, there is evidence that children experiencing severe poverty are more likely to experience persistent rather than short-term poverty (Adelman *et al.*, 2003). However, for the majority of children, the poverty experience is short term (Jenkins and Rigg, 2001). Bradbury *et al.* (2001) found that, of those children who were in the bottom fifth of the income distribution in the first year studied, 77 per cent had moved up the income ladder by the fifth year. This may be related to age and because they are being replaced by younger generations who are particularly vulnerable.

We can see from Table 11 that younger children (aged nought to four) are more likely than average to be recurrent and long-term persistent poor, whereas older children (aged ten to 15) are more likely to be short-term persistent poor or one-off poor (Jenkins and Rigg, 2001). Similar results have been found elsewhere. For example, Hill and Jenkins (2001) found that young children, those aged nought to four in particular, were more likely than others in the population to be repeatedly poor, and Adelman *et al.* (2003) found that young children (aged nought to four) were disproportionately represented among the persistently and severe poor. Adelman *et al.* (2003) also demonstrated that the length of a poverty spell is generally greater and the level of its severity is generally worse in households with a large number of children; with no workers; in receipt of benefit; with at least one adult with a limiting illness; and with at least one adult of non-white ethnicity.

There is a chance that children on relatively high incomes will fall into poverty: Bradbury *et al.* (2001) found that 5 per cent of children in Britain in the middle fifth of the children's income distribution in one year were in the poorest fifth of the distribution in the next year. The entry rate to low income of those on the

Table 11 Poverty pattern over nine years for dependent children

Poverty pattern	All dependent children (%)	Age 0–4 (%)	Age 5–9 (%)	Age 10–15 (%)	All persons (%)
Proportion poor in wave 1 cross-section	25	28	26	21	20
Never	45	40	48	45	53
One-off	13	10	12	17	13
Recurrent[a]	7	11	6	3	6
Short-term persistent[b]	25	23	23	33	19
Long-term persistent[c]	10	16	11	2	8
Total	100	100	100	100	100

a Either observed poor at two interviews of poverty separated by at least one interview of non-poverty, or three to six interviews of poverty out of nine separated by at least two interviews of non-poverty.
b Either two consecutive interviews poor, or three to six interviews of poverty separated by at most one interview of non-poverty.
c Poor at seven or more interviews out of nine.

Source: Jenkins and Rigg (2001).

middle rung of the ladder was 13 per cent five years later. But there was also a fair amount of churning within the low-income groups. Adelman *et al.* (2003) used the BHPS to investigate the persistence of *severe* income poverty.[1] They demonstrated that . the vast majority who experienced *severe* poverty during the five-year period studied had just one spell (91 per cent) – when they left severe poverty they did not return to severe poverty again within the five-year period of childhood. Nevertheless, the route out of *severe* poverty was only to the next rung of the ladder to non-severe poverty rather than to non-poverty, and children who left *non-severe* poverty were more likely to return to it. Routes into severe poverty were as likely to be sudden and straight from non-poverty as they were to be gradual via non-severe poverty. For children, it is relatively easy to slide into severe poverty but climbing the ladder back out again is relatively difficult.

Jenkins and Rigg (2001) identified four main events that can act as ladders or snakes into poverty for families with children. These are income from benefits; non-benefit, non-labour income (i.e. maintenance for lone parents); income from employment; and household change. These will be dealt with in turn.

Income from benefits

Changes to the tax and benefit package for children have been instrumental in New Labour's aim to reduce the number of children in low-income households by at least a quarter by 2004 as a contribution towards the broader target of halving child poverty by 2010 and eradicating it by 2020. Between 1998/99 and 2001/02, there was a fall in the relative child poverty rate after housing costs of 10 per cent and before housing costs of 16 per cent.[2] The Government claimed that the reforms introduced from 1997–2001 would reduce the number of children in poverty by 1.2 million (HM Treasury, 2001). But the *HBAI* figures up to 2000/01 showed that the reduction in child poverty had been only 500,000 (DWP, 2002b). Three main factors account for this difference in result. First, the poverty figures were still out of date – covering only six months after the introduction of Working Families' Tax Credit (WFTC). Second, there is a problem of non-take-up of both WFTC and Minimum Income Guarantee (MIG). Third, the Government has been chasing a moving target – the 60 per cent of median threshold has been moving upwards as a result of real increases in the incomes of the better off (Brewer *et al.*, 2002).

There have been significant changes in the child tax and benefit package since 2001/02. This has led the Government to report that, by April 2003, because of personal tax and benefit measures, households with children would on average be £1,200 per year better off; and those in the poorest fifth of the population would on average be £2,500 better off a year in real terms compared with 1997 (DWP, 2002c). The new tax credit system is expected to make up any losses suffered by families with children (particularly affecting lone-parent families) as a result of policy changes since 1997 (Sutherland, 2002).

The most recent estimates of the impact of tax and benefit policy changes introduced between 1997 and 2003/04 are that, other things being equal, they would have reduced child poverty by about 1.3 million children. However, because other things were not equal – in particular, average incomes increased and thereby raised the poverty threshold – there were about one million fewer children in poverty in 2003/04 compared with 1997 (Sutherland et al., 2003).

The new tax credit system

The new tax credit system comprises two new tax credits: the Child Tax Credit and the Working Tax Credit, which were introduced from April 2003. The Child Tax Credit brings together different elements of support for children previously paid via Income Support, Jobseeker's Allowance, Working Families' Tax Credit; Disabled Person's Tax Credit and the Children's Tax Credit to create a seamless system of financial support for children, which will be paid to both working and non-working parents. The Working Tax Credit is a means-tested supplement to low wages, for which childless couples and single people over 25 as well as families with children are eligible. Therefore adult- and child-related support has been separated while, at the same time, support for children of working and non-working parents has been integrated. The new tax credits intend to build on previous efforts to lift children out of poverty via promoting employment and increasing income.

The Child Tax Credit provides considerably more generous payments than the benefits it replaces. The rates of benefits for out-of-work families will be equalised with the benefits or tax credits for in-work families. Child benefit will be disregarded as income for Income Support purposes, which has boosted the income of some of the poorest families (Ridge, 2003). Also, the credit will be paid to the main carer, normally the mother, rather than through the wage packet, which addresses 'purse versus wallet' concerns that money paid directly to the mother is more likely to be spent on children, whereas money paid to the father will be spent on himself (Goode *et al.*, 1998; Ridge, 2003). The approximate net gain from the new system of tax credits will be £6 a week for the first child. The amount of £54.25 per week for a first child is guaranteed for all families with an income of less than £13,000 per year.

Taking the new tax credit system into account, Sutherland (2002) demonstrated (using the tax-benefit model Polimod)[3] that the effect of the 2003/04 policy regime on the poverty rates of children in lone-parent families is dramatic, compared with simulation results for previous regimes. Compared with 1997, child poverty rates fall by eight percentage points (on an AHC basis) from 35 per cent to 27 per cent. Thus 1.06 million children are taken out of poverty. On a BHC basis, the scale of poverty reduction is larger: 1.28 million children or a reduction of 37 per cent.

The 2003/04 regime is estimated to have resulted in 26 per cent fewer children in lone-parent families in poverty and 22 per cent in two-parent families. Table 12 shows the chances of escaping poverty between the 1997 and 2003/04 policy regime for lone-parent families. For lone-parent families, the changes in policy have enabled a much higher proportion of children under three and children with parents in paid work for at least 16 hours a week to climb out of poverty. For children in large lone-parent families, and children of teenage parents (whose parent was under 20 when their first child was born), benefit income policy was also a

60

Table 12 Children in lone-parent families: risk of poverty and chances of escaping poverty by characteristics

Children below the poverty line	1997 policies		2003/04 policies		% reduction
	Number (000)	%	Number (000)	%	
Age of child					
0–2	350	79	170	39	50
3–4	270	75	200	57	24
5–10	800	71	600	54	25
11–15	550	64	460	53	16
16–18	120	45	110	41	9
Gender of parent					
Female	1,970	70	1,450	52	27
Male	110	53	100	48	9
Number of children in family					
1	430	51	370	44	15
2	770	68	570	50	26
3	890	82	610	57	31
Age of parent when first child born					
Under 20	610	85	430	60	30
20–25	840	78	610	57	77
25+	640	50	510	41	19
Employment status of parents					
Not in paid work	1,630	88	1,260	68	23
Paid work <16 hours	130	80	120	70	13

(Continued)

61

Table 12 Children in lone-parent families: risk of poverty and chances of escaping poverty by characteristics *(continued)*

Children below the poverty line	1997 policies		2003/04 policies		% reduction
	Number (000)	%	Number (000)	%	
Paid work 16–29 hours	220	55	120	30	45
Paid work 30+ hours	110	17	50	9	49
Other adults in the household?					
No	1,850	72	1,370	53	26
Yes	240	50	180	38	23
Of which:					
None aged 16–21	60	40	40	28	30
Some aged 16–21	170	55	140	43	21
All	2,080	68	1,550	51	26

Note: The poverty line is 60 per cent of the within-scenario median equivalised household income.

Source: Sutherland (2002).

particularly effective ladder out of poverty. Reductions are smaller than average for children in the oldest age group, sole children, children with parents in paid work for less than 16 hours and children living with non-dependent older siblings (aged 16 to 21).

The evidence indicates that tax and benefits act as a ladder out of poverty for children, but to different extents depending on the circumstances of the child. Tax and benefits are therefore selective ladders.

Child support as a ladder

The Child Support Agency (CSA) was designed to increase the number of maintenance awards. But the overall proportion of lone parents who reported receiving maintenance remained unchanged during the first two years of the Child Support Agency's operation. In 2001, only 31 per cent of lone parents received child maintenance (Table 13). This is an increase from 25 per cent in 1999 but remains unchanged compared to the 1994 figures (Marsh and Perry, 2003).

While private transfers (including maintenance) account for only 6 to 7 per cent of total income, 'a little goes a long way'. Boheim *et al.* (1999) concluded that receipt of maintenance appears to make a substantial contribution to lone mothers' living standards. They sampled lone mothers who started receiving

Table 13 Receipt of child support 1999–2000: lone mothers

	1999 (%)	2000 (%)	2001 (%)
No order or agreement	53	53	51
Order or agreement, not paid	22	20	18
Paid	25	27	31
	100	100	100
Unweighted base	2,131	1,874	1,837

Source: Marsh and Perry (2003).

maintenance over two consecutive years and those who stopped receiving maintenance. When lone mothers started receiving maintenance, their level of total gross monthly household income rose substantially, from £726 to £867 – indicating that the absolute amount of, for example, earnings also rose. But, when looking at those lone mothers who stopped receiving maintenance, household income fell substantially, from £932 to £753 a month.

The level of maintenance received varies by type of lone parent (Table 14). Marsh and Perry (2003) found that formerly married lone mothers receive the most. Compared with 1994, the amounts received by formerly married lone mothers kept up with wage inflation, or better. But the amounts reported by single, never partnered lone mothers began smaller and remained unchanged.

There is also evidence that maintenance payments reduce hardship only if they increase income and are not offset by a fall in benefit (Bryson et al., 1997). Marsh et al. (1997) demonstrated that those receiving both Family Credit and maintenance payments had equivalent incomes 60 per cent higher than those on Income Support who received no maintenance payments. The £15 that Family Credit recipients were then allowed to keep made an important difference.

It is not merely the receipt of maintenance or the amount received that is important, but also that the source of income is

Table 14 Amounts of child support: by type of lone parent – total amounts

Mean amounts per month	1994 (£)	1999 (£)	2000 (£)	2001 (£)
Ex-married	45	57	67	70
Ex-cohabitation	34	33	39	42
Single	27	31	31	32
All	39	54	56	57

Source: Marsh and Perry (2003).

regular. There is evidence that the average length of period that lone parents are in receipt of maintenance is short. Marsh and Perry (2003) demonstrated that, over a three-year period, 37 per cent of lone mothers received some maintenance in one of those three years but only 13 per cent received it for all three years. On the other hand, spells of non-receipt are relatively long. Boheim *et al.* (1999) modelled entry to and exit rates from maintenance. They predicted that one-half of lone mothers receive maintenance for less than 2.3 years, while one-half of women experience a period of non-receipt for more than 8.7 years. A lone mother can expect to receive maintenance only 23 per cent of her time as a lone mother (Boheim *et al.*, 1999). But, as we have seen, her poverty status relies on this source of income.

There is evidence that maintenance payments can be a ladder into work; just under half of those in work receive child support payments compared to 17 per cent not working/working fewer than 15 hours a week (Marsh and Perry, 2003). This is not necessarily because those out of work have partners who are less likely to pay, nor is it because child support opens up ways to pay for childcare (Marsh *et al.*, 1997; Marsh and Perry, 2003). Rather, maintenance acts as an extra source of income that enables lone parents to manage on smaller earnings for shorter hours (Marsh *et al.*, 1997), making combining work with looking after children a financially viable option.

Reform of the child support system is a key area in New Labour's fight against child poverty. The aim is that it should contribute to the reduction of child poverty by achieving a rise in the proportion of parents meeting their financial obligations to their children. But there is a shortfall between the actual cost of children and the percentage system that calculates non-resident parents' maintenance liability (Ridge, 2003). Also, the newly introduced £10 disregard for children whose resident parent is on Income Support or Job Seeker's Allowance applies only to cases assessed under the new formula, leaving about 400,000 persons with care, and their children, not gaining from this (Ridge, 2003). Time will tell whether the reforms mean that maintenance serves as a more effective ladder out of poverty for children in lone-parent families.

Child support as a snake

Although the receipt of child support can act as a ladder for the resident parent, the payment of child maintenance can be a snake for non-resident parents. Maintenance payments can reduce the non-residential father's second family to social assistance levels (Van Drenth *et al.*, 1999). The legislation gave biological fathers an obligation to maintain their children. The long-established practice by which the state assumed that the man would maintain his second family while it would support the first was formally abandoned (Van Drenth *et al.*, 1999). The child support system thus increased required payments by non-residential fathers to their biological child and no allowance was made for their second family's children, who would suffer as a consequence. Only from 1995 was allowance made for some travel-to-work costs and contact costs for the non-residential parent.

The recent reform to some extent tries to account for this. Those with a net income of up to £200 a week pay less and those with net incomes of up to £100 a week or who are on benefit pay only £5 a week. Only in other exceptional cases, where the non-resident parent has certain specified child-centred expenses, will the rates be lowered. This includes a non-residential parent's commitment to non-biological or biological children in a new marriage or cohabitation. The non-resident parent is now able to reduce his financial liability to his biological child on the basis of the other children in his home.

However, even the flat rate of £5 per week may cause hardship for families managing on severely restricted budgets (Ridge, 2003). Indeed, up to 40 per cent of non-resident parents are expected to have higher assessments under the new scheme compared with the old one, and 70 per cent of these will be low-income parents receiving less than £200 per week (CPAG, 2000). Also, allowance is no longer made for the non-resident parent's housing costs. This could have negative effects on the living standards of the children in these families.

Paid work as a ladder

It is well established that worklessness is related to income poverty and hardship (Ermisch et al., 2001; Vegeris and McKay, 2002; Adelman et al., 2003). As we have seen, families with very young children, and especially children in lone-parent families, are more likely to be poor (Piachaud, 2001). Children in lone-parent families are at a much lower risk of poverty if the lone parent is employed full time (Bradshaw, 2002; Kemp et al., 2002). But lone-parent families are less likely to be in any kind of paid work: the proportion of worklessness among lone-parent households with dependent children is much higher than the working-age population in general, at 44 per cent in spring 2002, although this is ten percentage points lower than in 1992. As with all mothers, the economic activity rate of lone mothers increases with the age of the youngest child.

To alleviate child poverty, New Labour's aim is to increase the employment rate of lone-parent families to 70 per cent by 2010. Whether this target can be achieved on recent trends is questioned by Berthoud (2003a) who estimated that about 62 per cent of lone parents would be employed by 2010 and that 70 per cent would not be reached until 2015, although this does not take into account the likely impact of planned policy developments over the next few years (Millar, 2003). Recent work by Sutherland (2002) demonstrates that, for the target to be achieved, all lone parents with children over three would have to move into paid work and that, in order to achieve the goal of halving child poverty for children in lone-parent families, these lone parents would have to enter 30-hour minimum wage jobs; 16-hour minimum wage jobs are not sufficient. The alternative is higher-paid jobs (Sutherland, 2002).

An important question to ask is whether work is sufficient in itself as a ladder out of poverty. Vegeris and McKay (2002) undertook useful analysis on changes in hardship that coincide with changes in families' work status. Both lone parents and couples scored lower in hardship when they became full-time employed families in 2000. Indeed, severe hardship rates were two-thirds lower for full-time working lone parents and 50 per cent lower for full-time couples who were not working in 1999. As Chapter 3 showed, full-time work is an important ladder out of poverty.

Work is not a ladder for everyone and continuous work does not necessarily protect children from (persistent and/or severe) poverty (Adelman et al., 2003). Moreover, childcare costs can significantly reduce the financial returns from working, especially for people who are low paid. The typical cost of a nursery place for a child under two is now £128 a week or more than £6,650 a year. This compares to the average weekly household income of £550 and average weekly spending on food and housing combined of £77.60 (Daycare Trust, 2003). On average, parents pay three-quarters of the cost of childcare in the UK, with the Government paying most of the rest through the Childcare Tax Credit plus a small contribution by employers. The current average award through the Childcare Tax Credit of £40.61 a week is less than a third of the typical cost of a nursery place (Daycare Trust, 2003).

The burden of childcare costs for lone-parent families is demonstrated by Polimod simulation undertaken by Sutherland (2002), in which she estimated the effect of different levels of childcare costs on the gain from taking paid work for 30 hours on the national minimum wage (Table 15). A low-cost childcare scenario assumes childcare costs of £20 a week with the actual cost for parents being £6 out of their in-work income after the Childcare Tax Credit is taken into account. The high-cost scenario assumes childcare costs at the maximum level for support; £135 for one child (actual cost is £94.50) and £200 for two (actual cost is £140). Out-of-pocket expenses are assumed to be £40.50 and £60 respectively.

Table 15 Increase in income for lone-parent families who enter work under 2003/04 tax-benefit policies

Gain per week	No childcare costs (%)	Low childcare costs[a] (%)	High childcare costs[b] (%)
Worse off	0	Neg[c]	44
Under £10	Neg[c]	1	6
£10–20	1	3	20
£20–30	1	9	10
£30–40	3	19	4
£40–50	22	24	4
£50–70	45	21	4
£70–100	14	12	4
£100–150	11	7	4
£150+	4	3	Neg[c]
Mean gain	£67.95	£56.77	–£2.55
Median gain	£56.31	£47.67	£9.41

a Assumes childcare costs of £20 a week with the actual cost for parents being £6 after Childcare Tax Credit.
b Assumes childcare costs at the maximum level for support; £135 for one child (actual cost is £94.50) and £200 for two (actual cost is £140).
c Neglible.
Source: Sutherland (2002).

The gain from taking paid work is estimated to fall a little under the low-cost scenario (compared to if there are no childcare costs). The high-cost scenario leads to an estimated 44 per cent of job entrants becoming worse off in paid work – the out-of-pocket cost of childcare exceeds the gained income from paid work. Moreover, this does not include out-of pocket work expenses, which may lower disposable income significantly. High childcare costs, even with state support, are a trigger into poverty for a large proportion of working (lone) parents.

Farrell and O'Connor (2003) found that having older children who could look after themselves or inexpensive (or free) childcare arrangements meant higher discretionary income, even if earnings were relatively low.

Ladders into work

Childcare

New Labour's National Childcare Strategy is an integral component of the package of government policies tackling child poverty both directly and indirectly.

First, childcare can enable mothers, especially lone mothers, to take up paid work. A significant proportion of lone parents (although not couple families) cite a lack of affordable childcare as a reason for not working (Marsh, 2001). However, only a minority identify childcare as the sole barrier and lone parents long established in work rarely cite childcare as a major difficulty that they had to overcome to enter and/or to keep paid work. Childcare allows a decision to work to be enacted, it neither allows the decision itself nor creates the working opportunity. But it is still important, and additional provision at the right time will more quickly ease the move into work (Marsh, 2001).

The National Childcare Strategy has created more childcare places, mainly in the form of funding for nursery classes in primary schools – all children aged three and four are now guaranteed a part-time place in pre-school education (and the 2004 Budget announced a pilot to extend this guarantee to 6,000 two year olds living in disadvantaged areas). But it is arguable that this, mainly part-time, term-time provision, is not the most effective way of enabling (poor) lone parents to obtain access to employment (Bradshaw and Bennett, 2003). Also, provision is mainly targeted at the 20 per cent most deprived wards, but campaigners have called for comprehensive provision, pointing out that two-thirds of children living in poverty do not live in the most disadvantaged areas (Daycare Trust, 2002b). But, despite the shortcomings of the National Childcare Strategy, the increase in available childcare in deprived areas can help to provide affordable childcare to enable parents to move from unemployment into work.

Second, childminding offers scope to build on acquired life experience and to combine working with parenting, making it a potential source of employment for lone parents. But, for the move from Income Support to childminding to be a ladder and not a snake requires specialist, integrated and continuing assistance. Without this, it may result in failure, leaving the lone parent in a burden of debt and the prospect of continuing poverty for their own children (Bond and Kersey, 2002). Moreover, childminding often offers poor and unpredictable wages, especially in areas of disadvantage where shift work and temporary jobs are common, and lone parents will lose many benefits on entering work (Bryson et al., 1997). But, if the move is successful, they will be able to establish ladders out of poverty for themselves as well as the parents and children who use the services (Bond and Kersey, 2002). However, it is unlikely that the supply of childminding is sustainable because, while demand for care work of all kinds is increasing, the supply of labour for this work is shrinking. This is because of changing demographics;

increased employment opportunities offering flexible working patterns; a lack of support for childminding at the local authority level; low pay and poor status of the work; and the exploitation of those doing childminding (Mooney *et al.*, 2001).

The expansion of childcare has been a step towards a ladder into employment (and out of poverty) for families with children, especially lone parents. But childcare in the UK is still seen primarily in the context of parents' opportunities for employment, and is still expensive (Daycare Trust, 2003) and largely market orientated. This is one reason why we still have a relatively low proportion of lone parents in employment and a relatively high proportion of children living in workless households. It has been argued that the Government will not be able to meet its target of eliminating child poverty within 20 years without universal childcare provision (Land, 2002).

Welfare-to-work policies

Welfare-to-work initiatives aimed specifically at families with children can lower the first rung of the ladder. New Labour has introduced a variety of welfare-to-work incentives such as the New Deals – especially relevant to families with children is the New Deal for Lone Parents (NDLP). NDLP is a voluntary programme aimed at all non-employed lone parents and those working for less than 16 hours a week, regardless of age of children or of receipt of Income Support. But those with children over three are targeted. Each lone parent who participates in NDLP is allocated to a New Deal Personal Adviser who offers information, advice and support, and can offer specific help with finding jobs in childcare and training.

NDLP appears to facilitate entry into work, and subsequently acts as a potential ladder out of poverty. Research[4] shows that it impacts significantly on Income Support exits, and that the likelihood of moving into work from the programme is highest in the first 30 days of participating and the subsequent two-month period. The first two months of participation results suggest an additional 25 per cent of exits from Income Support as a result of NDLP (Evans *et al.*, 2003). Participants were more likely than non-participants to have entered full-time work at a nine-month point of evaluation; to report job satisfaction; to report job stability; and to believe that they would still be in the particular job in 12 months' time (Evans *et al.*, 2003). Given the importance of childcare for lone parents accessing work, it is also useful to know that the NDLP reduced the number of childcare barriers for participants (Evans *et al.*, 2003). The NDLP is therefore a useful ladder into work and potentially out of poverty.

But only a small minority of lone parents on Income Support actually participate in NDLP (around 6 to 7 per cent) and therefore the overall effect of NDLP on reducing the total Income Support population is very small (Lessof *et al.*, 2001). The probability of participation decreases with each additional child and on the presence of young children, especially babies and infants (Lessof *et al.*, 2003). According to quantitative analysis, ethnicity appears to have no impact on participation in NDLP. However, qualitative research suggests that minority ethnic lone parents experience barriers to participation in NDLP, such as language problems and subsequent misunderstanding of the letter inviting them to an NDLP interview (Dawson *et al.*, 2000; Pettigrew, 2003)

Household change: ladders

While children in lone-parent households are the most likely to be poor, they do not usually live in a lone-parent family for the whole of their childhood. About half of those who become lone parents will have found a partner within six years (McKay, 2003). For lone parents, repartnering is one important way to climb out of poverty (Jenkins and Rigg, 2001). Lone parents moving from a lone-parent to a couple status between 1999 and 2000 on average gained a 28 per cent increase in their income (Vegeris and McKay, 2002). If repartnering is combined with an increase in workers, then poverty is virtually eliminated (Jenkins and Rigg, 2001). Marsh and Perry (2003) found that eight out of ten lone parents on Income Support (IS) leave IS if they repartner. But, as McKay (2003) has demonstrated, leaving lone parenthood does not affect the employment status of the lone parent. Rather, lone parents are partnering with someone who is already working.

However, repartnering is relatively rare (Jenkins and Rigg, 2001). Indeed, Adelman et al. (2003) showed that, while the transition between moving from a couple to a lone parent is relatively frequent (8 per cent of children), only 1 per cent moved from living in a lone-parent to a couple household.

Jenkins and Rigg (2001) identified a fall in the number of children as being the most effective trigger for an exit from poverty for couples with children. This is because, when a child leaves home, this potentially frees up income that can be spent on other children in the family. In Jenkins and Rigg's study, this has been captured by the change in the household's equivalence scale rate. A child leaving home can also increase household income by opening up time for parents, especially mothers, to move into paid work. But, if the child had been employed or had some other income, this could lead to a fall in household income and could thus trigger a fall into poverty. For the child who leaves home, this event is likely to lead to a short-term, dramatic drop of income while perhaps studying away from home, working for low pay or on benefits, etc. (Adelman et al., 2003).

Household change: snakes

The very act of having a child can be a snake into poverty. A significant minority (one in three) of households experience a fall in living standards on the birth of a baby and up to one in six (between 10 and 15 per cent) fall into poverty as a result (HM Treasury, 1999b). This can be a result of a variety of needs that arise when a baby is born – such as a bigger house and certain major items. If the child is born to a teenage parent, there is a greater chance of poverty. Teenage parenthood has serious long-term consequences, not only for the teenage mother's employment and income opportunities, but also for her child/ren (Bradshaw and Bennett, 2003).

Many children are born into pre-existing poverty; their parents (and other children in the family) are already living in poverty when they are born. Both the pre-existing financial situation of parents and the impact of early parenthood on family finance need to be taken into account in order to establish effective ladders out of poverty for babies and the associated unequal life chances (Bennett, 2002). But some state financial support exists for each (additional) baby born. Some of these initiatives are relatively new and the effect on child poverty is yet to be seen, although there is the potential to simulate the effects of these using, for example, Polimod.

Having an *additional* child, especially if the family already has two, can slide a family into poverty; children in large families are more likely to suffer from poverty. It has been demonstrated, using a hardship measure of deprivation, that larger families experience greater hardship, especially in the transition between two and three-plus families (Vegeris and McKay, 2002; Willitts and Swales, 2003). Adelman *et al.* (2003) demonstrated (as shown in Table 16) that, over a five-year period, three in ten children in persistent and severe poverty (28 per cent) and one-quarter of

Table 16 Changes in the number of children in the household by poverty status

	Persistent and severe poverty (%)	Persistent poverty only (%)	Short-term and severe poverty (%)	Short-term poverty only (%)	No poverty (%)	All children (%)
Same number of children in household all years	58	58	53	60	70	64
Decrease in number of children in household	(8)	13	25	19	13	14
Increase in number of children in household	28	24	(16)	16	15	18
Both increase and decrease	(7)	6	(6)	5	2	4
Total	100	100	100	100	100	100

() = less than 20 unweighted cases.

Columns may not sum to 100 because of rounding errors.

Source: Adelman *et al.* (2003).

children in persistent poverty only (24 per cent) had experienced new children joining the household, either because of a birth or stepchildren being added to the pre-existing family, compared with only one in seven not in poverty (15 per cent). It is estimated that over half of all children in low-income families by 2004 will be in large families (DWP, 2002c).

In larger families, there is a greater likelihood that one parent is out of employment; the number of children, rather than the age of the youngest, is becoming more important in influencing mothers' labour market participation rates (Davies and Joshi, 2001; Willitts and Swales, 2003). The reasons for this need to be investigated but it may be because work for mothers with a large number of children does not pay – a result of the high cost of childcare, which, especially if children are born close together, can be a huge additional expense for families with a larger number of children (Bennett, 2002). Indeed, the maximum amount of financial help available under the Childcare Tax Credit for two children is not double that of one child and therefore, for large families in particular, a move from benefits into work is likely to be a snake into poverty. But the practicalities of transporting children to and from different childcare providers (including school) may detract mothers from working since this is more difficult to organise with a larger number of children, especially if the children are with different providers (Skinner, 2003).

Bradshaw (2002) points out that the UK tax benefit package generally is doing considerably less for large low-paid working families than it does for large families on Income Support. Since 1997, Child Benefit, one of the few mechanisms within the financial support system that attempts to level out the income between families without children and families with children, has been increased in real terms by 29 per cent for the first children but only by 5 per cent for second and subsequent children (Piachaud, 2001).

A fall in the number of children can, at least in the short term, act as a snake into poverty. Adelman *et al.* (2003) showed that a fall in the number of children increased the risk of short-term poverty; a quarter of children in short-term and severe poverty (25 per cent) had experienced a decrease in the number of children in the household. This could either be because a dependent child had left home resulting in a subsequent loss of benefits or because an ill or disabled child had died, depending on the ratio of costs and benefits.

There has been little research on the effect that a death of a child has on child poverty. Corden *et al.* (2001) undertook an in-depth study of the financial implications of the death of a child. They found that the cessation of benefits (which families with an ill or disabled child rely heavily on) caused a move into financial hardship largely because of short- to medium-term financial costs – such as funeral expenses – that families experience after the death of a child. However, a fall in the number of children does not appear to be a snake into poverty long term (Adelman *et al.*, 2003).

An adult falling ill or disabled can also trigger a fall into poverty. Children in families with an adult with a illness that limited their daily activities are more likely to be poor and, the longer they live in these circumstances, the worse their poverty experience generally is. According to Adelman *et al.*'s (2003) study, more than half (56 per cent) of children in persistent poverty had lived with an ill adult for at least one year during the five-year period studied, compared to one-quarter (26 per cent) of children who had experienced no poverty. One in ten children in persistent poverty had spent the entire five-year period living with an adult with an illness that limited their daily activities.

Children who live for a long time with a continuously ill adult are somewhat better off than those who live with an adult who is ill for only three or four years, or those who live with an adult who moves in and out of ill health, as shown in Table 17 (Adelman *et al.*, 2003).

Table 17 Adult illness transitions and child poverty (percentages)

	Persistent and severe poverty	Persistent poverty only	Short-term and severe poverty	Short-term poverty only	No poverty	All children
No years with ill[a] adult	44	44	67	59	74	62
Always at least one ill adult	(10)	8	(6)	(4)	3	5
No ill adults to ill adults	14	14	(6)	12	7	10
Ill adults to no ill adult	(11)	9	(9)	7	4	6
Two or more transitions	21	26	(12)	18	12	17
Total	100	100	100	100	100	100

a An illness that limited their daily activities.

Unweighted base: 2,103.

() = less than 20 unweighted cases.

Columns may not sum to 100 because of rounding errors.

Source: Adelman et al. (2003).

This suggests that the benefits system better protects children living with a long-term ill or disabled adult than those living with an adult who moves in and out of illness.

A child being born/falling ill or disabled can result in a significant decrease in disposable income for a family. Excluding food, parents spend on average a fifth of their income a week on a disabled child and the average *additional* cost compared to a non-disabled child is £99.15 per week at 1997 prices (Dobson and Middleton, 1998). A severely disabled child would cost parents at least three times as much as a child without a disability, if the goods and services regarded as essential were all being purchased (Dobson and Middleton, 1998).

The benefits system acknowledges that disabled children incur additional financial costs as a result of their disabilities, mainly through Disability Living Allowance (DLA) and the disability premium in Income Support. But research by Dobson and Middleton (1998) found that benefits fall far short of what parents believe to be the minimum essential costs for severely disabled children. The shortfall varied between 20 per cent for a child aged between six and ten years who cannot walk and almost 50 per cent for children aged five years or less, regardless of their disability. For these families, even if children were receiving their maximum entitlement, benefits would need to be increased by between £30 and £80 per week in order to meet the minimum essential costs identified by parents.

Since the Dobson and Middleton (1998) study was carried out, benefits for disabled children have been improved. The Welfare Reform and Pensions Act 1999 extended the DLA higher rate mobility component to disabled three and four year olds. This came into effect in April 2001 and is worth an extra £37.40 per week. It was expected to benefit some 8,000 children. April 2001 also saw the disabled child premium in Income Support increase to £30 per week (up by 35 per cent) and the carer's premium increase to £24.40 per week. Those with a child getting higher rate DLA care now get an additional £11.05 a week. In addition, a disabled Child Tax Credit worth an extra £30 per week for working parents was introduced, paid through Working Families' Tax Credit or Disabled Person's Tax Credit. For parents with a severely disabled child (defined as in receipt of DLA care component at the highest rate), there was an additional £11.05 per week. These are significant extra weekly amounts.

Yet the increase in benefits has not provided an adequate ladder out of poverty for many families with disabled children. The 2000 General Household Survey shows that, for both boys and girls, the presence of a limited long-standing illness is higher in the lower socio-economic groups compared to the top socio-economic groups (Beresford, 2002), and two in three families with disabled children are in the bottom 40 per cent income band, despite changes to disability benefits and initiatives to encourage parents back to work (Prasad, 2002). Of all families who care for disabled children, 55 per cent either are or have been living in poverty (Sharma, 2002). The 3 per cent of the child population who are disabled are more likely to be born into poorer families (Prasad, 2002).

While benefits for families with disabled children may still be too low, low take-up is also a problem. Reith (2001) points out that promotion and increase of take-up of DLA is crucial in raising the income of families with a disabled child – accessing DLA could be worth an additional £159.40 a week for a family on Income Support (Reith, 2001).[5] April 2003 saw the introduction of the Child Tax Credit, which is paid at a higher rate if the child has a disability and at an enhanced rate for a child with a severe disability. The effect of this on poverty for families with disabled children remains to be seen.

Poverty among disabled children also arises because the parents of disabled children are less likely to be in work and are less likely to be in full-time work than are parents of non-disabled children (Prasad, 2002). This is partly because disabled children are more likely to be living in a lone-parent family (Reith, 2001). Lone-parent families with disabled children face the same problems as other lone parents in combining work with raising children but face huge additional problems. The cost of childcare, not wanting to leave their child with a stranger, lack of accessible childcare places, all combine to make it very unlikely that a lone parent with a disabled child will be able to work (Reith, 2001). They therefore do not access the in-work benefits and do not access the benefits of income from work.

Ladders into work for parents of disabled children include more flexible specialist childcare, and community-based play and leisure facilities. The services currently available are for short breaks rather than after-school care. Until April 2003, the Childcare Tax Credit was payable only for care with registered providers outside the child's home. This excluded the many parents with a disabled child who cannot find accessible, appropriate childcare outside their home or those for whom it is in the child's best interests to be cared for in their own home. As from April 2003, the Childcare Tax Credit was extended to cover childminders approved to care for children in their parents' own home, domiciliary workers or nurses from a registered agency who are approved to provide care in the parents' own home. But, because the Child Tax Credit still does not take into account the higher costs of specialised childcare, it is questionable whether the extension of the Childcare Tax Credit to include childcare in the home will actually have a significant impact on the poverty rates for families with disabled children.

Key points

The key points to emerge in this chapter are as follows.

- There are events that push children into severe poverty with relative ease but finding ways to lift them out again is relatively difficult.

- Overall, changes to the tax and benefit package have enabled children to climb out of poverty, depending on the circumstances of the child.

- Maintenance payments can be a ladder out of poverty and into work (by acting as a wage supplement) if they are regular and not offset by a fall in benefit.

- Paid work can be an important ladder out of poverty for families with children.

- Repartnering, especially if the new partner is in work, is an important ladder out of poverty for lone parents.

- The death of a child can push a family into short-term poverty as a result of financial expenses and benefit withdrawal.

- The benefit system has acted as a protective factor in preventing children living in a family with a continuously ill disabled adult from falling into poverty, but is less good at protecting families with adults moving in and out of illness.

- Higher benefits, increased take-up and better financial support for specialist childcare would help to lift more families with disabled children out of poverty.

6   OLDER PEOPLE

Snakes and ladders are a better descriptor of the income changes that affect working-age adults and children than they are for older people. For most older people,[1] the level and source of their income in retirement is determined by their opportunities in working life (Ginn and Arber, 1996). Indeed, Bardasi *et al.* (2002) implicate changes that occur just before retirement age in determining post-retirement-age poverty. They also found that retirement itself could be a snake – in 1999, 26 per cent of the retired compared with only 12 per cent of the non-retired and 5 per cent of workers were poor (living on incomes below two-thirds of the 1991 median) and there was no improvement of the chances of being poor in retirement in successive cohorts.

Income changes in older age occur less often and usually less precipitously for pensioners than for other groups. For those who receive it – almost all men over retirement age, but only half of all women – the Basic State Pension provides a protective cushion to changes to other income sources. The limited research on this subject tends to focus on income changes rather than poverty *per se*. However, given the proximity of much of the pensioner population to low income, the two factors are clearly strongly linked. This chapter explores evidence on income mobility in old age and what is known about specific snakes and ladders.

According to the 2001 Census, just over a fifth of the UK population (5.3 million women and 6.9 million men) were aged over 60. The older share of the population over retirement age is growing as life expectancy increases and the larger birth cohorts enter retirement. The highest rate of growth is in the 75 and older age group, which also contains the poorest pensioners – mainly women, because of differential mortality rates (Walker *et al.*, 2001). Increases in relationship breakdown and single living will also result in more older poorer women.

Life expectancy has been increasing at a faster rate than healthy life expectancy. In consequence, average years spent in, and aggregate rates of, ill health will increase. Where ill health brings higher costs, it will be a causative snake towards poverty. This is especially the case where ill health is associated with non-take-up of benefits. Although limiting ill health is not the inevitable consequence of advanced age, the association is undeniable. Figure 2 shows that, as people age, limiting ill health increases. The decline in male ill health past age 85 is probably explained by differential mortality rather than individual pensioners

Figure 2 Limiting illness and age

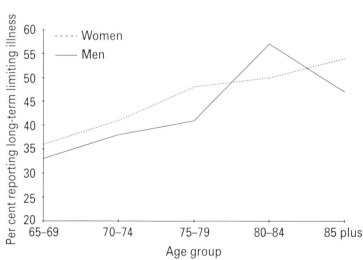

Source: Bridgwood (2000, p. 34, Table 13). Data is for Great Britain.

actually getting healthier. Ill health is also segmented by income level: the poor suffer the greatest ill health (Marmot *et al.*, 2003). This suggests that the increased costs of ill health are disproportionately borne by those least able to afford such extra costs.

Associated with ageing is the question of who is to be expected to pay for dependency in old age. It is clear that older people are being expected to contribute to the costs of some community care services out of their incomes. Average- and low-income pensioners already find it difficult to pay for care services in their own homes. People also overestimate their retirement incomes and do not understand how long-term care is financed, thinking that the Government can and should pay for it (Deeming and Keen, 2002).

Also relevant are the trends in housing tenure over the last quarter of the twentieth century, away from renting and towards owner-occupation. The highest rates of home ownership are in the working-age population (Table 18). As these cohorts age, more and more older people will own their own homes. In terms of their wealth, the post-war baby boomers did well out of the housing market, but most of their assets are tied up in bricks and mortar. Such assets cannot easily be liquidated. Older people need somewhere to live, may be attached to the 'family' home and may resist selling a family asset. Some of these future retirees may be asset rich but cash poor. This will have implications for their consumption, quality of life and ability to maintain their homes in a decent state of repair. Hancock (1998) investigated the scope for equity relief in relieving poverty. She found the scope for equity relief was limited and restricted mainly to the oldest age group who are most likely to be poor, but it could not provide much benefit to those in the greatest poverty. However, the benefits of equity release for some of the oldest home owners are not insignificant.

Table 18 Housing tenure by cohorts (percentages)

	45–54	55–59	60–64	65–74	75–84	85 plus
Social renters	16	16	19	24	29	34
Private renters	6	5	5	4	6	7
Owner occupiers	77	79	76	72	65	59

Columns may not sum to 100 because of rounding errors.

Source: National Statistics (2003, Table 4.3). Data is for Great Britain.

As a whole, the older population has done well out of post-war economic growth compared to older people in the past. Rising affluence, more valuable state benefits (including SERPs), sustained full employment (prior to the mid-1970s) and the development of occupational pensions have all disproportionately benefited the old and those approaching old age. On average, the older population has become comparatively richer and moved up the income distribution in the last 20 years. But this hides substantial and growing inequality within the group. Younger-couple pensioners, owner-occupiers and those with private pensions have generally done well. But older pensioners, single women and tenants either with little or no occupational or private pensions or savings remain concentrated at the base of the income distribution (Figure 3).

As may be seen in Figure 3, very few older people reported incomes below about £70 per week (in 2001/02). This is the protective impact of the Basic State Pension, though the level may be low and, arguably, inadequate (Parker, 2000). Figure 3 also shows that most pensioners are bunched in the lower part of the distribution, well below the mean. There is also a small but very long upper tail of pensioners reporting very substantial incomes. There are many implications from the distribution for the study of poverty. First, bunching in the lower part of the distribution means that, if one uses a proportion of the mean or median as a poverty measure, the numbers classified as poor

Figure 3 Income distribution, families with one or more member aged 60-plus

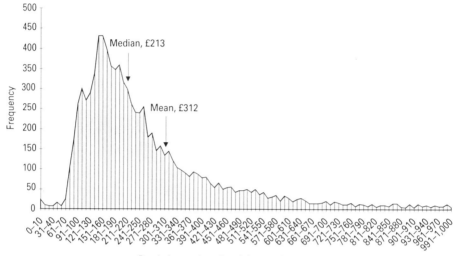

Banded gross benefit unit income (£ per week)

Reproduced from Dornan (2004). Data is from the Family Resources Survey collected in 2001/02 for Great Britain.

will be very sensitive to the threshold chosen. Second, it shows how little separates people near to the bottom of this income distribution. This also means that the key anti-poverty policy, the income-tested Pension Credit (which replaced Income Support/ Minimum Income Guarantee in October 2003) will bring larger proportions of pensioners into entitlement, if not necessarily receipt, of means-tested benefits.

Table 19 gives current indicators of poverty levels using *HBAI* data. The *HBAI* definition is based on a proportion of the prevailing median. As the table shows, there is little difference in the *HBAI* poverty rates before and after housing costs. Single female pensioners have higher poverty rates. There was a fall in pensioner poverty between 1997 and 2003/04: it fell by one million pensioners when measured on after-housing costs and only a quarter of a million before housing costs (Sutherland *et al.*, 2003).

Figure 4 shows which income sources are most important by decile. It illustrates just how reliant most pensioners are on the Basic State Pension. The amount of pension is broadly constant across the deciles but is proportionately more important for the

Table 19 Poverty rates among pensioners (percentages)

	Pensioner couples	Single male pensioners	Single female pensioners	Whole population
HBAI 60% of median (BHC), 2001/02	22	17	24	17
HBAI 60% of median (AHC), 2001/02	22	18	24	22

Source: DWP (2003a, Table D5.1)

Figure 4 Sources of income in retirement by income decile

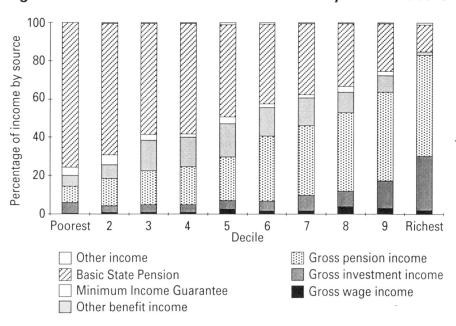

Reproduced from Dornan (2004). Data is for Great Britain in 2001/02.

poorest since they have so little other income. Figure 4 also illustrates how limited, as a group, is the importance of means-tested and disability benefits ('other benefit income'). These make a big difference to recipients but are claimed by a small proportion of the population. Changes in the Minimum Income Guarantee and Pension Credit will increase the proportions in receipt of these benefits and the importance of these income sources (especially, but not exclusively for the poorer deciles).

Income mobility in later life

More research is now available on income mobility, thanks mainly to the maturing of the British Household Panel Survey. A study that drew on the Retirement Survey and used two time-points (1988–89 and 1994) reported that incomes over the five-year span had experienced little overall change (Johnson *et al.*, 1998). It found a bunching of individuals in plus or minus 10 per cent change over this period, ranging from 57.4 per cent for unmarried women, 56.2 per cent for existing widows, 48.5 per cent for single men, 48.0 per cent for married men and 33.0 per cent for married women. It found much higher mobility for those who suffered bereavement, with the death of a husband costing each family £50 per week on average (in January 1996 prices). In this study, the researchers used data for recent retirees only. Although *a priori* logic would suggest that this group would face the greatest (downward) mobility, they tended to be both richer than predecessor cohorts (more to lose) and to derive more income from less stable (private) income sources. As Figure 4 illustrates, income source varies substantially by income position: the poor are reliant on state benefits but the rich derive much of their income from non-state sources. Since benefit levels are stable or increasing (at least in comparison to prices), the poor are, to a degree, insulated against income change. Their income may be low, and even inadequate, but it is relatively stable.

Studies using rather more time-points (from the British Household Panel Survey) have suggested higher levels of mobility. Zaidi *et al.* (2001), Zaidi (2001) and Dornan (2004) found higher levels of mobility. Zaidi *et al.* (2001) suggest that, although income is less volatile for older than for younger people, it would be wrong to suggest that they are stable.

Zaidi *et al.* (2001) categorise the British Household Panel Survey by type of income trajectory (Table 20). The first column in Table 20 refers to rank position (hence movement within a population) and the second to absolute movement (compared to previous income). On the rank measure, only one-third of older people experienced no change in position. A further 16 per cent experienced a blip, but over half experienced sustained (rising or falling) or significant (that is, multiple) changes in income. When one uses an absolute measure, mobility looks much higher (only

Table 20 Income mobility trajectories in old age, 1991–97

Trajectory	Description	15 percentage shift in rank position	15 percentage shift in income
Flat	No significant move	30.4	11.9
Rising	Significant, sustained, upward movement in at least one year	12.3	17.7
Falling	Significant, sustained, downward movement in at least one year	11.2	4.9
Blip	A fall followed by rise or rise followed by fall and no other change	16.1	12.5
Zigzag	Multiple changes	30.0	53.1

Source: Zaidi *et al.* (2001, Tables 4 and 5). Data is from BHPS for Great Britain.

one in ten shows a flat trajectory and over half show repeated movement).

One of most important aspects to low income that longitudinal research has uncovered is that, although aggregate rates of poverty may appear relatively constant from year to year, the group has a high turnover. Jarvis and Jenkins (1997) analysed the first four waves of the BHPS for all age groups. They found that, of those defined as in poverty (defined as on or below half the wave 1 mean income) in wave 1, 46 per cent had left by wave 2 and 78 per cent by wave 3. This suggests both a comparatively small group that endures persistent poverty and that poverty entry and exit rates are high. There appears to be a poverty periphery – a group close to poverty who may fall into it but may also subsequently escape. Of the group Jarvis and Jenkins defined as initially poor, 31 per cent were pensioners: of those who had escaped by the fourth year, 28 per cent were pensioners. Over the same period, 20 per cent of pensioners had entered poverty. The poor population has a high turnover and the older population are part of this. Therefore, it ought not to be assumed that, once in poverty, individual pensioners will remain in the same position in the next year.

Predictors of income change

Cohort effects

Younger pensioners, and those approaching retirement tend to have higher incomes and assets than the older generations they follow (Johnson and Stears, 1998). Either successive cohorts of pensioners are getting richer (because of greater lifetime earnings and assets accrual) or incomes shrink after retirement (e.g. through capital dis-saving) or because the balance of the cohort changes with poorer women outliving richer men. Johnson and

Stears (1998), exploring male income only, find age-related reductions in labour income and slight reductions also in social security payments. They also find that, generally, younger male pensioners have higher private pension and investment income than older pensioners, but suggest that the effect is predominantly explained by greater private pension coverage and asset accrual of later cohorts rather necessarily than capital dis-saving or under-indexation of pensions. The conclusion needs testing – the authors used cross-sectional data for men only from the Family Expenditure Survey, when longitudinal data would have been better – but, if true, this result is rather encouraging, as it suggests that successive cohorts will not only retire richer but will also retain much of this additional income through their retirement.

Employment

Employment income for the older population is important for a relatively small number of pensioners. These pensioners tend to be younger (close to State Pension Age) and often richer. Smeaton and McKay (2003) used combined Family Resources Survey data from 1997–2000 to examine employment rates in Great Britain beyond the state pension age (Table 21). The English Longitudinal Study on Ageing (ELSA) found slightly different employment rates

Table 21 Employment rates beyond the state pension age (percentages)

Age group	Men	Women
60–64	–	25
65–69	13	8
70–74	8	3
75–79	4	2

Source: Smeaton, and McKay (2003, Table 2.2).

in England for men and women beyond state retirement age (Banks and Casanova, 2003). However, both studies indicate that a significant minority of people who are beyond retirement age continue in paid employment, though the rates tail off quite quickly after five years.

In population terms, this income source is insignificant (it comes under 'other income' in Figure 4), but, to those in employment (predominantly younger couples and richer), the source is important and volatile. It also it falls in value as people age, especially for unmarried men (Johnson *et al.*, 1998). Johnson *et al.* (1998) used Family Expenditure Survey data (from the 1960s to the 1990s) to create various cohorts of those born between 1890 and 1919. They found that average labour market income declined for each age cohort. Zaidi (2001), using BHPS data for 1991–97, suggested that the chances of downward mobility were about three times greater for those retiring than for those already retired. Presumably, those already retired had already undergone this downward mobility. Leaving work (whether above or below the state pension age) is clearly associated with substantial, but possibly predictable, income reduction.

Investment income

Figure 4 shows that investment income is not particularly important on average. Nevertheless, it has become more important over the post-war period and a greater source of income instability than in previous generations. Although it is mainly the rich who derive the most income from equities, the very poor (decile 1) also appear to get proportionately more of their income from this source than deciles 2 to 6. This is probably the effect of some asset-rich, income-poor pensioners being excluded from some means-tested benefits because of their capital holdings.

Zaidi (2001) found that investment income is associated with short-range income mobility, thereby increasing the chances of older men's income reducing and pensioners' income not increasing. This suggests that income from investments does not offer much security of income. Disney *et al.* (1998) used Retirement Survey data, for those close to the state retirement age, to explore the life-cycle savings hypothesis, that is, the extent to which capital is built up prior to and around retirement and then subsequently dis-saved. They found that it tended to occur partly through active behaviour and partly through the way in which the annuity market values the investments of individuals with different expected longevities. This conclusion appears to contradict previous work of two of the same authors (Johnson and Stears, 1998) using the same data source for male pensioners' capital, in which investment income did not de-accumulate in the way previously thought.

Bereavement

Perhaps the most important predictor of sudden household income change in old age – which may or may not lead to impoverishment – is the loss of a partner. Zaidi (2001) analysed the BHPS to explore this and found that bereavement was linked with upward income mobility. The reason for this probably lies with the technique of equivalisation, which seeks to adjust income by an indicator of 'need'. It values the same money income more highly for singles than for couples. Hence, no income change but the loss of a partner will show up as a large income increase. This effect will be present only when income and wealth are actually inherited by a spouse, but we know that this is not always the case for private pensions. If a loss in pension is experienced, then downward income mobility is likely. This will disproportionately affect women since they tend to be both survivors and those without the separate pensions rights. Indeed Dornan (2004) uses the first ten waves of the BHPS (up to 2001) to show that household change – predominantly bereavement – is strongly associated with coming into receipt of an assistance benefit (MIG), which is itself a predictor of poverty.

Benefit take-up

Official estimates for 2000/01 suggested that, of those entitled, one in three pensioners failed to claim MIG, one in ten did not claim and nearly two in five failed to claim Council Tax Benefit (DWP, 2003b). Although the latest available estimates are rather dated, between two and three out of five entitled older people failed to claim their entitlement to Disability Living Allowance/ Attendance Allowance (Social Security Select Committee, 2000). Take-up rates of the new Pension Credit (launched in October 2003) are likely to be low. A large number of newly entitled pensioners will be drawn into an unfamiliar system and most will have relatively small entitlements to benefit. Most of these benefits go to the poorest and can improve their purchasing power and, through this, quality of life and health (see Craig et al., 2003). They offer a ladder out of extreme deprivation. Whether this adds up to a route out of poverty is arguable, but the level of means-tested benefit for pensioners has been increased very substantially in real terms since 1999.

Key points

The key points to emerge in this chapter are as follows.

- Income in later life is determined largely by opportunities in working life.

- Income changes in later life are less precipitous than for young groups in the population.

- But, even in later life, incomes are not stable: there is some movement into and out of poverty among older people.

- Those approaching retirement and young pensioners tend to have higher incomes and assets than the older generations they follow.

- The means-tested pension has increased substantially above the increase in average earnings in recent years, thereby enhancing its role as a ladder out of poverty; but a third of entitled pensioners do not claim it. An increase in benefit take-up will therefore help pensioners to escape from poverty.

7   Future research priorities

This report has reviewed the existing literature on ladders out of poverty. Chapter 1 of the report set out the background to the review. Chapter 2 briefly summarised existing statistical information on routes into and out of poverty. Chapter 3 reviewed the research evidence on paid work as a means of lifting people out of poverty. Chapters 4 to 6 focused on ladders out of poverty for children and families, young people and older people respectively. This final chapter builds on the earlier analyses to outline possible future research priorities for the Joseph Rowntree Foundation on ladders out of poverty.

Ladders out of poverty

Leaving aside education, the key ladders out of poverty identified in the review are:

1   paid work – moves into work or increased earnings

2   increases in non-labour income

3   changes in household composition

4   moves out of ill health or disability.

These are not self-contained categories. Moves into paid work, for example, may occur when a non-employed lone parent repartners with someone who is employed. However, in principle, the four potential ladders are separable, even if two or more may interact to help lift a household out of poverty. Hence, a programme of research could be structured around these four ladders and the interconnections between them (especially those between paid work and the other three ladders).

Although the research should be focused on the United Kingdom, there may be scope for a limited amount of comparative research where it is clear that lessons may be learned about routes out of poverty. This could include literature reviews as well as empirical research.

There is a significant gap in knowledge about routes into and out of poverty among minority ethnic groups, which requires urgent attention. There are also gaps in knowledge in relation to disabled people and carers. The gender dimension has also been neglected in recent years (Bradshaw *et al.*, 2003).

Paid work

The New Labour Government has argued that work is the surest and best route out of poverty. The evidence on poverty dynamics summarised in Chapter 2 certainly confirms that labour market events account for the largest share of exits from poverty. These labour market events include, not only movements from non-work into paid employment, but also increased earnings among people who are already employed. There is a need for more research on the factors that help to move people from unemployment and economic inactivity into paid work.

There is a particular need for research into the props that need to be in place for this ladder out of poverty to be effective. There is a growing body of knowledge on childcare, the New Deals and benefit rules that reduce the risk of transitions into work, but important gaps remain. For example, we do not know whether the provision of services such as affordable childcare is more or less important than financial support for children as a ladder out of poverty. In addition, more research is needed on other supports, both financial and practical, that need to be in place to help lone mothers move into paid employment.

Although work is the most important ladder out of poverty, it is not a guarantee. In particular, employment does not always protect children from poverty, especially when there is only one worker in the household. There needs to be greater understanding of when work acts as a ladder and when it acts as a snake, and the implications this has for children, especially in relation to the distribution of resources within the household. A qualitative study by Farrell and O'Connor (2003) was useful in that it looked at the effect of the transition from benefits to work on the resources distributed to children within the household. More research is needed like this, but in relation to other sources of income and not just earnings from paid work.

The New Labour Government has introduced a wide range of measures – such as the national minimum wage and the new Working Tax Credit – that aim to 'make work pay'. Nevertheless, there are a significant number of people in paid employment who are living in poverty. The number of working poor households would fall if the take-up of new tax credits were to increase. More research could therefore be undertaken on the obstacles to the take-up of the new tax credits (Working Tax Credit and Child Tax Credit) and innovative ways in which they could be overcome.

A more fundamental reason why work is not a guarantee of escaping poverty is that entry jobs tend to be low paid. Moreover, low-paid jobs do not necessarily lead onto better-paid ones. Earnings mobility is relatively limited in Britain. In addition, low-paid jobs are often followed by a return to unemployment, as people move between welfare and work and back again. More research is needed on why and how people get caught up in this 'no-pay, low-pay' cycle and what can be done to break it. For example, why do some people stay in work but others do not? We also need a better understanding of the mechanisms that generate the 'scarring' effect of unemployment on subsequent earnings. More research is also needed on the factors that promote job retention and that facilitate job advancement. Why are some people able to progress from low-paid to better-paid jobs while others do not?

While paid employment may be the best route out of poverty, there are some groups for whom it is less suitable or not appropriate at all. The dividing line between capacity and incapacity for work is somewhat fuzzy. It is also potentially contentious because it can have implications for benefit entitlement and whether or not claimants are required to look for work. However, there are some groups for whom work may not be a realistic proposition in the short term, even if it is viable in the medium or longer term.

With the partial exception of disabled people, relatively little research has been undertaken on how those at the margins of work can be supported and how realistic work is for them. These 'hard-to-employ' groups include the most severely disadvantaged homeless people and problem drug users (two groups that overlap but are not identical), as well as some people with mental health problems and others who are some distance from the labour market. In addition, further work needs to be done on routes into paid employment for people who are not economically active because of their unpaid caring responsibilities, such as people who are looking after disabled children or adults.

Non-labour income

Paid labour is not the only source of income that can help people to escape from poverty, nor is it all that relevant to some groups of people, such as those who have retired or are unable to work. Other sources of income are required to lift them out of poverty. In addition, non-earned income can help to make employment a more feasible proposition or, in combination with earned income, help to raise households out of poverty. Non-labour income includes:

- social security benefits and tax credits

- private and occupational pensions

- child support payments

- other private transfers.

One obvious source of non-labour income is social security benefits and tax credits. There has been a growing body of research modelling the impact of taxes and benefits on the number of children in poverty (e.g. Sutherland *et al.*, 2003). However, more research could be undertaken on what else could be done through the tax and benefit system to lift the remaining poor children out of poverty, including children in large families and those suffering from severe or persistent poverty. In addition, more research could be undertaken on the impact of state transfers on other groups including those without children, disabled people and pensioners.

Lone parents in receipt of maintenance are more likely to move into work than those who are not. Maintenance can also help to lift families out of poverty, but may have the reverse effect on second families of non-resident fathers who have repartnered. Research on the effect of the child support reforms (implemented in 2003) is needed. The Department for Work and Pensions is commissioning a series of projects on the new child support system, but there is scope for research that is independent of government. In particular, there is scope for research on the impact of the reforms on the financial well-being of both children living in lone-parent families and those living in the non-resident parent's second family. Research is also needed on the effects (including the effects on child poverty) of the introduction of sanctions for non-compliant, non-resident parents.

Non-resident parents and the poverty of children in their second families have been a largely neglected group, both in policy and research. However, the child support reform attempts to account for the poverty experienced in second families. The success of this needs to be evaluated by studying the impact of maintenance payments on these families before and after the reforms have been implemented. More generally, little is known about the poverty and well-being of children living in second families of non-resident parents.

Research is needed on ways to improve take-up of the new Pension Credit. This new scheme greatly increases the number of older people entitled to means-tested benefit. Success in encouraging newly entitled older people to claim will be critical to the success of the Credit. Research is also required on the effectiveness of Attendance Allowance at reaching those in need.

The literature has begun to explore the systematic disadvantaging of women that has pervaded the occupational, and state, pensions systems since the Second World War. Although Home Responsibilities Protection makes it easier for women to build up state pension rights, older single and widowed women suffer high rates of poverty. More research is needed on pensioner poverty and gender inequalities, focusing especially on independent pensions rights, divorce settlements and widows' inheritance of pensions rights.

The Stakeholder Pension has come under criticism for its voluntary nature, both in terms of employee and employer contributions. In considering whether to contribute to a Stakeholder, low-paid employees in effect have to choose between current spending and saving for their retirement: more poverty now versus less poverty later. The increased reliance on means testing in the Government's anti-poverty pensions policy and the apparent 'crisis' in personal and occupational pensions have pushed the incentive structure towards current consumption and away from saving for retirement. Research could be undertaken on the ways in which Stakeholder Pensions could be made to work more effectively to prevent future poverty in old age.

Household change

Many low-paid workers are not poor. This is because the incomes of other people in their household help to raise the total household income above the poverty line. This underlines the importance of household structures in considering routes into and out of poverty. Changes in household size or composition can help to lift people out of poverty (or push them into poverty). The kinds of demographic events that can affect the size or composition of households and their disposable income include:

- separation and divorce

- partnering or repartnering

- bereavement

- childbirth or addition of children to the household

- children leaving home

- arrival or departure of adults.

More research (both quantitative and qualitative) is needed on the implications of these demographic events on the number and type of households on routes into and out poverty. This includes research into how these demographic events affect income distribution within the household. Although an event may not change total household income, it may affect the way income is distributed within the household, which could have implications for the poverty experienced by individuals within it.

We know relatively little about how bereavement among working-age parents affects household disposable incomes and labour market attachment in the short and medium term. More in-depth research needs to be undertaken on the short- and long-term financial impact of the death of a child and the support parents have at this stage from services, benefits and employment. Research also needs to be undertaken that enables us to understand the financial impact of the death of a child on the children left behind.

More research is also needed on the financial implications of the birth of a child as a trigger into poverty for children, especially children in large families. This could examine both the impact of the birth of a first child on household poverty and intra-household poverty, and the impact of the second and subsequent births. The baby tax credit element of the Child Tax Credit provides extra help in the first year of a child's life, but we do not know how adequate this amount is in relation to the extra financial burden involved or how this varies between different types of household.

Young people are tending to live for much longer in their parental home (or return to it after graduation from university). They are also more reliant financially on their parents than previous generations. More research is needed into the material and financial support that some parents provide to young adults and the difference this makes, for example, in helping to keep them out of poverty or to get or retain paid work (and unpaid work placements that seem to be increasingly common).

Increases in lone parenthood, increased numbers of single-person households, smaller families and increased geographical mobility have all loosened intergenerational ties. Intergenerational cash transfers (at least from children to parents) are usually small/rare but help in kind ought not to be underestimated. With the post-war baby boom generation now approaching retirement, we have a cohort of older people that, although richer than its predecessors, may also have less familial support. This generation is likely to be rather active by previous standards (younger and healthier) but, as they age, the pressures of ensuring a sufficient income and quality of life for independent living may increase.

Health and disability dynamics

Changes in health or disability can act as both a snake into poverty and a ladder out of it. Although less common than income or demographic events, for the individual households concerned, they can be very important indeed. Research has shown that some people may move into or out of ill health, and disability status can also change over time (Burchardt, 2000).

Ill health and disability can affect people's capacity to do paid work and, by potentially affecting their eligibility or entitlement to benefit, their benefit income as well. There is a growing body of knowledge about pathways into and out of Incapacity Benefit, but relatively little about how changes over time in people's health or impairment(s) affect their incomes and act as snakes into or ladders out of poverty.

Having an adult moving in and out of ill health appears to affect the poverty of children more severely compared to those living with an adult who is ill or disabled long term. More research needs to be undertaken on the impact of the transition from good health to ill health (and visa versa) on child poverty, and specifically the role that the benefit system has during this transition.

The numbers of older people, especially old older people, are increasing, a trend that will continue as the post-war baby boom generation reaches retirement age and beyond. Not only will there be more older people but they will also live longer, suffer more ill health, and be more likely to live alone and far from their family. Many in this generation may be richer than their parents, but others will remain on low incomes. The impact of ill health and disability on the living standards of older people living in poverty deserves further research.

Key priorities for research

We have sketched out above a wide range of possible topics for future research on poverty snakes and ladders. But research budgets are more or less limited and consequently priorities have to be drawn up. Our shortlist for research priorities is set out below, based on important gaps in knowledge, the scale of the particular problem, what research is being done or known to be planned, and the practical realities of what can be achieved within the constraints of the LOOP programme.

1   *Paid work*: there is an urgent need for more research on job retention and advancement, and what can be done to tackle the 'no-pay, low-pay' cycle. Getting people into work via

programmes such as the New Deal is only half the story; helping them to stay in work and progress within the labour market is the important other half, about which much less is known. There is also an urgent need to further examine the barriers facing 'hard-to-help' groups and the problems that need to be addressed to enable them to move closer to the labour market. Very often, people in hard-to-help situations (such as homelessness, problem drug use, experience of being looked after) are not yet sufficiently close to the labour market to benefit from the New Deal and related welfare-to-work programmes.

2   *Non-labour income*: more research is urgently needed on what, in addition to improvements in pension entitlements, could be done to improve benefit and tax credit take-up. As we have seen, state income transfers can make an important contribution to lifting households out of poverty or at least reducing the extent of their poverty. This makes it all the more important that the take-up of social security benefits and tax credits is maximised. Much of the research on take-up has focused on social security benefits, but it is likely that the shift towards tax credits, and the wider eligibility for them compared with social security benefits, will have had an important influence on attitudes to take-up and the process of claiming. More research is also urgently required on the financial circumstance of non-resident parents and how the needs of their second families might be addressed.

3   *Household changes*: an important priority is the need to examine the impact on poverty and hardship of increases or decreases in the number of children in a household and the reasons for their arrival and departure. The financial impact

and consequences of bereavement is also a neglected and underestimated topic that requires further research. Although not about household change, we urgently need to know more about the needs of large families, how they cope financially and what more could be done to tackle the particular problems they face. More research is urgently required on the routes into and out of poverty of people from minority ethnic groups.

4   *Ill health and disability*: we urgently need to know more about why people with intermittent health problems and impairment appear to fare worse than those who face such problems in a more persistent form. We also need to know more about the financial consequences of ill health and impairment, and how they might be better recognised by the tax and benefit system.

Other people will come up with research priorities that may be different from what we see as the key issues. The fact that some topics have not been mentioned does not mean they are not important or should not have scarce research resources devoted to them. In searching out the underlying causes of poverty (and how people might be lifted out of poverty), it is most important to ensure that the research is methodologically rigorous, impartial and stands up to scrutiny within the limits imposed by the inevitable constraints of time, money and data availability.

NOTES

Chapter 2

1   Most of the income data referred to in this report has been equivalised using the McClements scale, which is the one used until very recently by the DWP. Different equivalence scales produce slightly different results. One weakness of almost all equivalence scales is that they do not take account of the extra financial needs incurred by disabled people (mainly because it is difficult to estimate those needs from survey data and they vary depending on the nature of the impairment). Consequently, the incidence of poverty among disabled people is almost certainly underestimated in poverty statistics.

2   The median is a measure of average income in which half the population are below and half are above that level.

3   Quintiles are points in the income distribution that divide the population into five equal-sized groups when ranked by size of income. The lowest income quintile group is the poorest 20 per cent of the population. The top quintile group is the richest 20 per cent of the population.

4   Since October 2003, the Minimum Income Guarantee has been called the Guarantee Credit element of the new Pension Credit.

Chapter 4

1   One-third of men and one-fifth of women live at home at the age of 25 (G. Jones, 2002).

Chapter 5

1   Children were considered to be experiencing persistent severe poverty if in poverty (between 27 and 59 per cent of the median) for three or more years, with at least one year in severe poverty (below 27 per cent of the median).

2   This is because, for those receiving Housing Benefit/ Council Tax Benefit, 85 per cent of the gains in income from Working Families' Tax Credit have been offset by losses in Housing Benefit and Council Tax Benefit. Only 220,000 WFTC recipients were getting Housing Benefit. Childless couples receive more Housing Benefit than couples with three children on the same earnings, who now pay a higher proportion of their gross rent.

3   Polimod calculates liabilities for, or entitlements to, income tax, National Insurance contributions (NICs), Child Benefit, Family Credit (FC), Working Families' Tax Credit (WFTC), Child Tax Credit (CTC), Income Support (IS) – including income-related Job Seeker's Allowance and pensioners' Minimum Income Guarantee, Housing Benefit and Council Tax Benefit.

4   The research tried to establish a counterfactual situation that replicates an identical situation but that did not have the NDLP in place, and then measured and compared the outcomes for the NDLP and non-NDLP situations. The 'treatment' and 'control' groups could not be randomly

assigned because the NDLP programme was rolled out nationally. Instead, a hypothetical comparison group using survey data was constructed.

5 DLA highest-rate care and mobility, carer premium, disabled child premium and enhanced disability premium.

Chapter 6

1 Broadly defined here as age 60 and over for both men and women, although different research drawn on uses different definitions.

REFERENCES

Acheson, D. (1998) *Independent Enquiry into Inequalities in Health*. London: HMSO

Adelman, L., Middleton, S. and Ashworth, K. (2003) *Britain's Poorest Children: Severe and Persistent Poverty and Social Exclusion*. London: Save the Children

Allen, T., Dobson, B., Hardman, J., Maguire, S., Middleton, S., Graham, J., Woodfield, K. and Maguire, M. (2003) *Education Maintenance Allowance Pilots for Vulnerable Young People and Childcare Pilots: Implementation and Reported Impacts in the First Year*. Research Brief No. 396. London: DfES

Anderson, I. (1999) 'Young single people and access to social housing', in J. Rugg (ed.) *Young People, Housing and Social Policy*. London: Routledge

Arulampalam, W. (2001) 'Is unemployment really scarring? Effects of unemployment experiences on wages', *The Economic Journal*, Vol. 111, November, pp. F585–F606

Ashworth, K., Hill, M. and Walker, R. (1994) 'Patterns of childhood poverty: new challenges for policy', *Journal of Policy Analysis and Management*, Vol. 13, pp. 658–80

Bane, M. and Ellwood, D. (1994) *Welfare Realities: From Rhetoric to Reform*. Cambridge, MA: Harvard University Press

Banks, J. and Casanova, M. (2003) 'Work and retirement', in M. Marmot, J. Banks, R. Blundell, C. Lessof and J. Nazroo *Health, Wealth and Lifestyles of the Older Population in England*. London: Institute for Fiscal Studies

Barclay, P. *et al.* (1995) *Joseph Rowntree Foundation Inquiry into Income and Wealth. Volume 1*. York: Joseph Rowntree Foundation

Bardasi, E., Jenkins, S. and Rigg, J. (2002) 'Retirement and income of older people: a British perspective', *Ageing and Society*, Vol. 22, No. 2, pp. 131–59

Bell, R. and Jones, G. (2002) *Youth Policies in the UK: A Chronological Map*. York: Joseph Rowntree Foundation

Bennett, F. (2002) *Giving All Children a Good Start: Financial Provision in Pregnancy and the First Year of Life*. London: Institute for Public Policy Research

Beresford, B. (2002) 'Children's health', in J. Bradshaw (ed.) *The Well-being of Children in the UK*. London: Save the Children Fund

Berthoud, R. (2003a) 'Lone parents and jobs – can the 70 per cent target be met?', in D. Thurley (ed.) *Lone Parents' Employment Target*. London: National Council for One-parent Families

Berthoud, R. (2003b) *Multiple Disadvantage in Employment: A Quantitative Analysis*. York: Joseph Rowntree Foundation

Bivand, P. (2003) *Reducing Child Poverty*. Working Brief 142. London: Centre for Economic and Social Inclusion

Blundell, R. and Walker, I. (2001) *Working Families Tax Credit: A Review of the Evidence, Issues and Prospects for Further Research*. London: Inland Revenue

Boheim, R., Ermisch, J. and Jenkins, S. (1999) *The Dynamics of Lone Mothers' Incomes: Public and Private Income Sources Compared*. London: Department of Social Security

Bond, M. and Kersey, D. (2002) 'Expanding childminding provision in areas of deprivation', *Local Economy*, Vol. 17, No. 4, pp. 303–12

Bradbury, B., Jenkins, S. and Micklewright, J. (2001) 'The dynamics of child poverty in seven industrialised nations', in B. Bradbury, S. Jenkins and J. Micklewright (eds) *The Dynamics of Child Poverty in Industrialised Countries*. Cambridge: Cambridge University Press

Bradshaw, J. (1999) 'Child poverty in comparative perspective', *European Journal of Social Security*, Vol. 1, pp. 383–406

Bradshaw, J. (2000) 'Prospects for poverty in Britain in the first twenty-five years of the next century', *Sociology*, Vol. 34, No. 1, pp. 53–70

Bradshaw, J. (2001) *Poverty: The Outcomes for Children*. London: Family Policy Studies Centre

Bradshaw, J. (2002) *Child Poverty and Large Families: A Research Note*. York: Social Policy Research Unit, University of York

Bradshaw, J. and Bennett, F. (2003) *Report on United Kingdom National Action Plan on Social Inclusion 2001–2003*. York: Social Policy Research Unit, University of York

Bradshaw, J. and Finch, N. (2002) *A Comparison of Chid Benefit Packages in 22 Countries*. Department for Work and Pensions Research Report 174. Leeds: Corporate Document Services

Bradshaw, J., Kemp, P.A., Baldwin, S. and Rowe, A. (2004) *The Drivers of Social Exclusion*. London: Social Exclusion Unit

Bradshaw, J., Finch, N., Kemp, P.A., Mayhew, E. and Williams, J. (2003) *Gender Poverty in Britain.* Manchester: Equal Opportunities Commission

Brewer, M., Clark, T. and Goodman, A. (2002) *The Government's Child Poverty Target. How much Progress has been Made?* IFS Commentary 88. London: Institute for Fiscal Studies

Bridgwood, A. (2000) *People Aged 65 and Over.* London: Office for National Statistics

Bryson, A., Ford, R. and White, M. (1997) *Making Work Pay: Lone Mothers, Employment and Well-being.* York: Joseph Rowntree Foundation

Burchardt, T. (2000) 'The dynamics of being disabled', *Journal of Social Policy*, Vol. 29, No. 4, pp. 645–68

Burgess, S. and Propper, C. (2002) 'The dynamics of poverty in Britain', in J. Hills, J. Le Grand and D. Piachaud (eds) *Understanding Social Exclusion.* Oxford: Oxford University Press

Bynner, J., Elias, P., McKnight, A. and Pierre, G. (2002) *Young People's Changing Routes to Independence.* York: Joseph Rowntree Foundation

Callender, C. and Kemp, M. (2000) *Changing Student Finances: Income, Expenditure and the Take-up of Student Loans among Full- and Part-time Higher Education Students in 1998/9.* London: DfEE

Coles, B. (1995) *Youth and Social Policy, Youth Citizenship and Young Careers.* London: UCL Press

Corden, A., Sainsbury, R. and Sloper, P. (2001) *Financial Implications of the Death of a Child.* York: Joseph Rowntree Foundation

CPAG (Child Poverty Action Group) (2000) 'Changes to the child support scheme', *CPAG Briefing*, March

Craig, G., Dornan, P., Bradshaw, J., Garbutt, R., Mumtaz, S., Syed, A. and Ward, A. (2003) 'Underwriting citizenship for older people: the impact of additional benefit income for older people', *Working Papers in Social Sciences and Policy*, No. 9, University of Hull

Davies, H. and Joshi, H. (2001) 'Who has borne the cost of Britain's children in the 1990s?', in K. Vleminckx and T.M. Smeeding (eds) *Child Well-being, Child Poverty and Child Policy in Modern Nations: What Do We Know?* Bristol: The Policy Press

Dawson, T., Dickens, S. and Finer, S. (2000) *New Deal for Lone Parents: Reports on Qualitative Studies with Individuals.* ESR55. Sheffield: Employment Service

Daycare Trust (2001) *Quality Matters.* London: Daycare Trust

Daycare Trust (2002a) *Childcare Costs Survey 2002.* London: Daycare Trust

Daycare Trust Press (2002b) Release, 6 November

Daycare Trust (2003) *Making Childcare Work: Changing Childcare for a Better Work–life Balance.* London: Daycare Trust

Dearden, C. and Becker, S. (2000) *Growing up Caring: Vulnerability and Transition to Adulthood – Young Carers' Experiences.* Leicester: National Youth Agency for the Joseph Rowntree Foundation

Deeming, C. and Keen, J. (2002) 'Paying for old age: can people on low incomes afford domiciliary care costs?', *Social Policy and Administration*, Vol. 36, No. 5, pp. 465–81

DfES (Department for Education and Skills) (2001) *Youth Cohort Study: The Activities and Experiences of 21 Year Olds: England and Wales 2000.* London: DfES

DfES (2003a) *Youth Cohort Study: The Activities and Experiences of 16 Year Olds: England and Wales 2002.* London: DfES

DfES (2003b) *Youth Cohort Study: The Activities and Experiences of 18 Year Olds: England and Wales 2002.* London: DfES

Dickens, R. (1998) 'Wage mobility in Great Britain', in J. Hills (ed.) *Persistent Poverty and Lifetime Inequality.* London: Centre for the Analysis of Social Exclusion, LSE and HM Treasury

Dickens, R. (1999) 'Wage mobility in Britain', in P. Gregg and J. Wadsworth (eds) *The State of Working Britain.* Manchester: Manchester University Press

Dickens, R. (2000) 'Caught in a trap? Wage mobility in Great Britain: 1975–1994', *Economica*, Vol. 67, pp. 477–98

Dickens, R. (2001) 'The national minimum wage', in R. Dickens, J. Wadsworth and P. Gregg (eds) *The State of Working Britain: Update 2001.* London: Centre for Economic Performance, London School of Economics

Dickens, R., Gregg, P. and Wadsworth, J. (2001) 'What happens to the employment prospects of disadvantaged workers as the labour market tightens?', in R. Dickens, J. Wadsworth and P. Gregg (eds) *The State of Working Britain: Update 2001.* London: Centre for Economic Performance, London School of Economics

Disney, R., Johnson, P. and Stears, G. (1998) 'Asset wealth and asset decumulation among adults in the Retirement Survey', *Fiscal Studies*, Vol. 19, No. 2, pp. 153–74

Dobson, B. and Middleton, S. (1998) *Paying to Care: The Cost of Childhood Disability.* York: Joseph Rowntree Foundation

Dornan, P. (2004) 'A failure to claim entitlements or to deliver rights? The non-take up of pension credit and older people', PhD thesis, University of York, York

Dorsett, R. (2001) *The New Deal for Young People: Relative Effectiveness of the Options in Reducing Male Unemployment.* PSI Research Discussion Paper 7. London: Policy Studies Institute

DWP (Department for Work and Pensions) (2002a) *Households Below Average Income 2001/2*. London: The Stationery Office

DWP (2002b) *Households Below Average Income 1994/5–2000/01*. Leeds: Corporate Document Services

DWP (2002c) *Opportunities for All: Fourth Annual Report 2002*. Cm. 5598. London: The Stationery Office

DWP (2003a) *Households Below Average Income 1994/5–2000/01: An Analysis of the Income Distribution from 1994/5–2001/02*. Leeds: Corporate Document Services

DWP (2003b) *Income Related Benefits Estimates of Take-up in 2000/2001 National Statistics*. http://www.dwp.gov.uk/asd/income_analysis/ tu0001.pdf (site visited May 2003)

DWP (2003c) *New Deal for Young People and Long-term Unemployed People Aged 25+: Statistics to March 2003*. London: DWP

Economic and Social Research Council (2001) *Children 5–16 Research Briefing Number 18 Poverty: The Outcomes for Children*. Swindon: Economic and Social Research Council

Erdem, E. and Glyn, A. (2001) 'Jobs deficit in UK regions', in R. Dickens, J. Wadsworth and P. Gregg (eds) *The State of Working Britain: Update 2001*. London: Centre for Economic Performance, London School of Economics

Ermisch, J. and Francesconi, M. (2001) 'Family matters: impacts of family background on educational attainments', *Economica*, Vol. 68, No. 270, pp. 137–56

Ermisch, J., Francesconi, M. and Pevalin, D.J. (2001) *Outcomes for Children of Poverty*. DWP Research Report No. 158. Leeds: Corporate Document Services

Evans, M., Eyrem, J., Millar, J. and Sarre, S. (2003) *New Deal for Lone Parents: Second Synthesis Report of the National Evaluation*. Leeds: Corporate Document Services

Farrell, C. and O'Connor, W. (2003) *Low-income Families and Household Spending*. DWP Research Report 192. Leeds: Corporate Document Services

Fieldhouse, E.A., Kalra, V.S. and Alam, S. (2002) 'A New Deal for Young People from minority ethnic communities in the UK', *Journal of Ethnic and Migration Studies*, Vol. 28, No. 3, pp. 499–513

Ford, J. (1999) 'Young adults and owner occupation: a changing goal?', in J. Rugg (ed.) *Young People, Housing and Social Policy*. London: Routledge

Ford, J., Rugg, J. and Burrows, R. (2002) 'Conceptualising the contemporary role of housing in the transition to adult life in England', *Urban Studies*, Vol. 39, No. 13, pp. 2455–67

Furlong, A. and Cartmel, F. (1997) *Young People and Social Change: Individualization and Risk in Late Modernity.* Buckingham; Philadelphia, PA: Open University Press

Gardiner, K. and Hills, J. (1999) 'Policy implications of new data on income mobility', *The Economic Journal,* Vol. 109, pp. F91–F111

Giddens, A. (1996) *In Defence of Sociology; Essays, Interpretations and Rejoinders.* Cambridge: Polity Press

Ginn, J. and Arber, S. (1996) 'Patterns of employment, gender and pensions: the effects of work history on older women's state pensions', *Work, Employment and Society,* Vol. 10, No. 3, pp. 469–90

Goode, J., Callender, C. and Lister, R. (1998) *Purse or Wallet?* London: Policy Studies Institute

Gordon, D., Adelman, L., Ashworth, K., Bradshaw, J., Levitas, R., Middleton, S., Pantazis, C., Patsios, D., Payne, S., Townsend, P. and Williams, J. (2000) *Poverty and Social Exclusion in Britain.* York: Joseph Rowntree Foundation

Gosling, A., Machin, S. and Meghir, C. (1996) 'What has happened to the wages of men since 1966?', in J. Hills (ed.) *New Inequalities: The Changing Distribution of Income and Wealth in the United Kingdom.* Cambridge: Cambridge University Press

Gossop, M., Marsden, J. and Stewart, D. (1998) *NTORS at One Year. Changes in Substance Use, Health and Criminal Behaviour One Year after Intake.* Wetherby: Department of Health

Gossop, M., Marsden, J. and Stewart, D. (2001) *NTORS after Five Years.* London: Department of Health

Gregg, P. (1998) 'The impact of unemployment and job loss on future earnings', in J. Hills (ed.) *Persistent Poverty and Lifetime Inequality.* London: Centre for the Analysis of Social Exclusion, LSE and HM Treasury

Gregg, P. and Pasanen, P. (2001) 'Entry wages since 1996', in R. Dickens, J. Wadsworth and P. Gregg (eds) *The State of Working Britain: Update 2001.* London: Centre for Economic Performance, London School of Economics

Gregg, P. and Wadsworth, J. (1996) 'More work in fewer households?', in J. Hills (ed.) *New Inequalities: The Changing Distribution of Income and Wealth in the United Kingdom.* Cambridge: Cambridge University Press

Gregg, P. and Wadsworth, J. (1999) 'Job tenure 1975–98', in R. Dickens, P. Gregg and J. Wadsworth (eds) *The State of Working Britain.* Manchester: Centre for Economic Performance, Manchester University Press

Gregg, P. and Wadsworth, J. (2000) 'Mind the gap, please: the changing nature of entry jobs in Britain', *Economica,* Vol. 67, pp. 499–524

Gregg, P. and Wadsworth, J. (2001) 'Everything you ever wanted to know about measuring worklessness and polarization at the household level but were afraid to ask', *Oxford Bulletin of Economics and Statistics*, Vol. 63, pp. 777–806

Gregg, P., Harkness, S. and Machin, S. (1999) *Child Development and Family Income*. York: Joseph Rowntree Foundation

Hancock, R. (1998) 'Can housing wealth alleviate poverty among Britain's older population', *Fiscal Studies*, Vol. 19, No. 3, pp. 249–72

Hendey, N. and Pascall, G. (2002) *Disability and Transition to Adulthood: Young Disabled People Speak*. Brighton: Pavilion Publishing

Higate, P. (2001) 'Suicide', in J. Bradshaw (ed.) *Poverty: The Outcomes for Children*. Occasional Paper 26. London: Family Policy Studies Centre

Hill, M.S. and Jenkins, S.P. (2001) 'Poverty among British children: chronic or transitory?', in B. Bradbury, J. Micklewright and S. Jenkins (eds) *Falling in, Climbing out: The Dynamics of Child Poverty in Industrialised Countries*. UNICEF

Hills, J. (1995) *Joseph Rowntree Foundation Inquiry into Income and Wealth. Volume 2: A Summary of the Evidence*. York: Joseph Rowntree Foundation

Hills, J., Le Grand, J. and Piachaud. D. (eds) (2002) *Understanding Social Exclusion*. Oxford: Oxford University Press

HM Treasury (1999a) *The Modernisation of Britain's Tax and Benefit System No. 5: Supporting Children through the Tax and Benefit System*. London: HM Treasury

HM Treasury (1999b) *Tackling Poverty and Extending Opportunity*. London: HM Treasury

HM Treasury (2001) *Tackling Child Poverty: Giving Every Child the Best Possible Start in Life*. London: HM Treasury

HM Treasury and DWP (2001) *The Changing Welfare State: Employment Opportunity for All*. London: HM Treasury and DWP

Hobcraft, J. and Kiernan, K. (1999) *Childhood Poverty, Early Motherhood and Adult Social Exclusion*. CASE Paper 28. London: Centre for Analysis of Social Exclusion, London School of Economics

Hodkinson, P. and Sparkes, A. (1997) 'Careership: a sociological theory of career decision making', *British Journal of Sociology of Education*, Vol. 18, No. 1, pp. 29–44

Jarvis, S. and Jenkins, S.P. (1997) 'Low income dynamics in 1990s' Britain', *Fiscal Studies*, Vol. 18, No. 2, pp. 123–42

Jarvis, S. and Jenkins, S.P. (1999) 'Marital splits and income changes: evidence from the British Household Panel Survey', *Population Studies*, Vol. 53, pp. 237–54

Jenkins, S.P. (2000) 'Modelling household income dynamics', *Journal of Population Economics*, Vol. 13, pp. 529–67

Jenkins, S.P. and Rigg, J.A. (2001) *The Dynamics of Poverty in Britain*. Department for Work and Pensions Research Report No. 157. Leeds: Corporate Document Services

Johnson, J. (2001) 'Child morbidity', in J. Bradshaw (ed.) *Poverty: The Outcomes for Children*. Occasional Paper 26. London: Family Policy Studies Centre

Johnson, P. and Stears, G. (1998) 'Why are older pensioners poorer?', *Oxford Bulletin of Economics and Statistics*, Vol. 60, No. 3, pp. 271–90

Johnson, P., Stears, G. and Webb, S. (1998) 'The dynamics of incomes and occupational pensions after retirement', *Fiscal Studies*, Vol. 19, No. 2, pp. 197–215

Jones, A. (2002) 'Homeless children', in J. Bradshaw (ed.) *The Well-being of Children in the UK*. London: Save the Children

Jones, G. (2002) *The Youth Divide: Diverging Paths to Adulthood*. York: Joseph Rowntree Foundation

Jones, G. and Wallace, C. (1992) *Youth, Family and Citizenship*. Buckingham: Open University Press

Kalra, V.S., Fieldhouse, E.A. and Alam, S. (2001) 'Avoiding the New Deal: a case study of non-participation by minority ethnic young people', *Youth and Policy. The Journal of Critical Analysis*, Vol. 72, pp. 63–80

Kellard, K. (2002) 'Job retention and advancement in the UK: a developing agenda', *Benefits*, Vol. 10, No. 2, pp. 93–8

Kemp, P.A. and Rugg, J. (1996) *The Single Room Rent: Its Impact on Young People*. York: Centre for Housing Policy, University of York

Kemp, P.A., Dean, J. and Mackay, D. (2002) *Child Poverty in Social Inclusion Partnerships*. Edinburgh: Scottish Executive

Kempson, E. (1996) *Life on a Low Income*. York: Joseph Rowntree Foundation

Kober, C. (2003) 'Baby bonds – can asset-based welfare tackle inequality?', *Poverty*, Vol. 115, Summer

Lakey, J., Barnes, H. and Parry, J. (2001) *Getting a Chance: Employment Support for Young People with Multiple Disadvantages*. York: Joseph Rowntree Foundation

Land, H. (2002) *Meeting the Child Poverty Challenge: Why Universal Childcare is Key to Ending Child Poverty*. London: Daycare Trust

La Valle, I., Finch, S., Nove, A. and Lewin, C. (2000) *Parents' Demand for Childcare*. DfEE Research Report 176. Nottingham: DfEE Publications

Leisering, L. and Leibfried, S. (1999) *Time and Poverty in Western Welfare States*. Cambridge: Cambridge University Press

Leisering, L. and Walker, R. (eds) (1998) *The Dynamics of Modern Society.* Bristol: The Policy Press

Lessof, C., Hales, J., Philips, M., Pickering, K., Purdon, S. and Miller, M. (2001) *New Deal for Lone Parents Evaluation: A Quantitative Survey of Lone Parents on Income Support.* ESR 101. Sheffield: Employment Service

Lessof, C., Miller, M., Philips, M., Pickering, K., Purdon, S. and Hales, J. (2003) *New Deal for Lone Parents Evaluation: Findings from the Quantitative Survey.* WAE147. Sheffield: Employment Service

MacDonald, R., Mason, P., Shildrick, T., Webster, C., Johnston, L. and Ridley, L. (2001) 'Snakes & ladders: in defence of studies of youth transition', *Sociological Research Online*, Vol. 5, No. 4, http://www.socresonline.org.uk/5/4/macdonald.html

McGlone, F. (2001a) 'Teenage pregnancy', in J. Bradshaw (ed.) *Poverty: The Outcomes for Children.* Occasional Paper 26. London: Family Policy Studies Centre

McGlone, F. (2001b) 'School exclusions', in J. Bradshaw (ed.) *Poverty: The Outcomes for Children.* Occasional Paper 26. London: Family Policy Studies Centre

McGlone, F. (2001c) 'Youth crime', in J. Bradshaw (ed.) *Poverty: The Outcomes for Children.* Occasional Paper 26. London: Family Policy Studies Centre

McGlone, F. (2001d) 'Children's smoking behaviour', in J. Bradshaw (ed.) *Poverty: The Outcomes for Children.* Occasional Paper 26. London: Family Policy Studies Centre

McGlone, F. (2001e) 'Adolescent alcohol use', in J. Bradshaw (ed.) *Poverty: The Outcomes for Children.* Occasional Paper 26. London: Family Policy Studies Centre

McGlone, F. (2001f) 'Drug use among children and young people', in J. Bradshaw (ed.) *Poverty: The Outcomes for Children.* Occasional Paper · 26. London: Family Policy Studies Centre

Machin, S. (1998) 'Intergenerational transmissions of economic status', in J. Hills (ed.) *Persistent Poverty and Lifetime Inequality.* London: Centre for the Analysis of Social Exclusion, LSE and HM Treasury

McKay, S. (2002) *Low/moderate Income Families in Britain: Work, Working Families Tax Credit and Childcare in 2000.* DWP Research Report No. 161. Leeds: Corporate Document Services

McKay, S. (2003) 'The dynamics of lone parents, employment and poverty in Great Britain', *Sociologia e Politica Sociale*, No. 2

McKnight, A. (2002) 'Low-paid work: drip-feeding the poor', in J. Hills, J. Le Grand and D. Piachaud (eds) *Understanding Social Exclusion.* Oxford: Oxford University Press

McRae, S. (1999) 'Introduction', in S. McRae (ed.) *Changing Britain: Families and Households in the 1990s*. Oxford: OUP

Maguire, S. and Maguire, M. (2003) *Implementation of the Education Maintenance Allowance Pilots: The Third Year, 2001/2002*. Research Report RR395. London: DfES

Marmot, M., Banks, J., Blundell, R., Lessof, C. and Nazroo, J. (2003) *Health, Wealth and Lifestyles of the Older Population in England*. London: Institute for Fiscal Studies

Marsh, A. (2001) 'Helping British lone parents get and keep paid work', in J. Millar and K. Rowlingson (eds) *Lone Parents, Employment and Social Policy: Cross-national Perspectives*. Bristol: Policy Press

Marsh, A. and Perry, J. (2003) *Family Change 1999–2001*. DWP Research Report 180. Leeds: Corporate Document Services

Marsh, A., Ford, R. and Finlayson, L. (1997) *Lone Parents, Work and Benefit: The First Effects of the Child Support Agency to 1994*. DSS Research Report 61. Leeds: Corporate Document Services

Mental Health Foundation (1996) *Joint Policy Statement on Race and Mental Health, A Briefing from the Mental Health Foundation*. London: Mental Health Foundation

Metcalf, D. (2002) 'The national minimum wage: coverage, impact and future', *Oxford Bulletin of Economics and Statistics*, Vol. 64, pp. 567–82

Middleton, S., Ashworth, K. and Braithwaite, I. (1997) *Small Fortunes: Spending on Children, Childhood Poverty and Parental Sacrifice*. York: Joseph Rowntree Foundation

Millar, J. (2003) 'Work as welfare? Lone mothers, social security and employment', paper presented at FISS conference, Sigtuna, Sweden

Millar, J. and Ridge, T. (2001) *Families, Poverty, Work and Care: A Review of Literature on Lone Parents and Low-income Couple Families*. DWP Research Report No. 153. Leeds: Corporate Document Services

Millar, J. and Rowlingson, K. (eds) (2001) *Lone Parents, Employment and Social Policy*. Bath: Department of Social and Policy Sciences, University of Bath

Mooney, A., Knight, A., Moss, P. and Owen, C. (2001) 'A profile of childminding: implications for planning', *Children and Society*, Vol. 15, No. 4, pp. 253–62

National Statistics (2002) *Population Report*. http://www.statistics.gov.uk/census2001/downloads/pop2001.xls (site visited May 2003)

National Statistics (2003) *Family Resources Survey*. London: DWP

Neale, J. (2002) *Drug Users in Society*. Basingstoke: Palgrave

New Earnings Survey (2003) London: Office for National Statistics

Nickell, S. (1996) 'The low-skill low-pay problem: lessons from Germany for Britain and the US', *Policy Studies*, Vol. 17, No. 1, pp. 7–21

Nickell, S. and Quintini, G. (2002) 'The recent performance of the UK labour market', *Oxford Review of Economic Policy*, Vol. 18, No. 2, pp. 202–20

Office of National Statistics (ONS) (1998) *Labour Force Survey 1997/98*. London: The Stationery Office

ONS (2004) *Labour Market Trends*, Vol. 112, No. 1. London: The Stationery Office

Palmer, G., Rahman, M. and Kenway, P. (2002) *Monitoring Poverty and Social Exclusion 2002*. York: Joseph Rowntree Foundation

Palmer, T. (2001) *No Son of Mine! Children Abused through Prostitution*. London: Barnardo's

Parker, H. (ed) (2000) *Low Cost but Acceptable Incomes for Older People*. London: Age Concern England and The Family Budget Unit.

Patsios, D. (2000) *Poverty and Social Exclusion Amongst the Elderly*. Working Paper 20. Poverty and Social Exclusion Survey of Britain and Townsend Centre for International Poverty Research. http://www.bris.ac.uk/poverty/pse/work_pap.htm (site visited May 2003)

Pavis, S., Platt, S. and Hubbard, G. (2000) *Young People in Rural Scotland: Pathways to Social Inclusion and Exclusion*. Work and Opportunity Series No. 17. York: Joseph Rowntree Foundation

Paxton, W. (2003) *Tax Efficient Saving: The Effectiveness of ISAs*. London: Institute for Public Policy Research

Pettigrew, N. (2003) *Experiences of Lone Parents from Minority Ethnic Communities*. Department for Work and Pensions Research Report No. 187. Leeds: Corporate Document Services

Piachaud, D. (2001) *Child Poverty, Opportunities and Quality of Life*. London: The Political Quarterly Publishing Company Ltd

Piachaud, D. and Sutherland, H. (2001) 'Child poverty in Britain and the New Labour Government', *Journal of Social Policy*, Vol. 30, No. 1, pp. 95–118

Pleace, N., Jones, A. and England, J. (2000) *Access to General Practice for People Sleeping Rough*. York: Centre for Housing Policy, University of York

Popham, I. (2003) *Tackling NEETs, Research on Actions and Other Factors that can Contribute to a Reduction in the Numbers of Young People not in Education, Employment or Training*. Connexions Research Report No. CNX R 01 2003. Connexions National Evaluation and Research Strategy

Powers, D.A. (1996) 'Social background and social context effects on young men's idleness transitions', *Social Science Research*, Vol. 25, pp. 50–72

Prasad, R. (2002) 'Breaking point', *Guardian Society*, 28 August

Quiglars, D. (2001a) 'Childhood accidents', in J. Bradshaw (ed.) *Poverty: The Outcomes for Children*. Occasional Paper 26. London: Family Policy Studies Centre

Quiglars, D. (2001b) 'Child abuse', in J. Bradshaw (ed.) *Poverty: The Outcomes for Children*. Occasional Paper 26. London: Family Policy Studies Centre

Quiglars, D. (2001c) 'The environment', in J. Bradshaw (ed.) *Poverty: The Outcomes for Children*. Occasional Paper 26. London: Family Policy Studies Centre

Quiglars, D. (2001d) 'Child homelessness', in J. Bradshaw (ed.) *Poverty: The Outcomes for Children*. Occasional Paper 26. London: Family Policy Studies Centre

Quiglars, D. (2001e) 'Educational attainment', in J. Bradshaw (ed.) *Poverty: The Outcomes for Children*. Occasional Paper 26. London: Family Policy Studies Centre

Quiglars, D. (2001f) 'Mental health', in J. Bradshaw (ed.) *Poverty: The Outcomes for Children*. Occasional Paper 26. London: Family Policy Studies Centre

Reith, L. (2001) 'Children, poverty and disability', *Poverty*, Vol. 109, Summer

Ridge, T. (2003) 'Labour's reforms of social security provision for families', *Benefits*, Vol. 37, No. 11, pp. 2, 86–92

Robinson, P. (1999) 'Education, training and the youth labour market', in R. Dickens, P. Gregg and J. Wadsworth (eds) *The State of Working Britain*. Manchester: Centre for Economic Performance, Manchester University Press

Rugg, J. (1999) 'The use and "abuse" of private renting and help with rental costs', in J. Rugg (ed.) *Young People, Housing and Social Policy*. London: Routledge

Rugg, J. and Burrows, R. (1999) 'Setting the context: young people, housing and social policy', in J. Rugg (ed.) *Young People, Housing and Social Policy*. London: Routledge

Scott, J. and Bergman, M. (2002) *Teenagers at Risk: Overcoming Family Disadvantage, Youth, Citizenship and Social Change Research Programme*. Research Briefing No. 15. Swindon: Economic and Social Research Council

Sharma, N. (2002) *Still Missing Out? Ending Poverty and Social Exclusion: Messages to Government from Families with Disabled Children*. London: Barnardo's

Shaw, A., Walker, R., Ashworth, K., Jenkins, S. and Middleton, S. (1996) *Moving off Income Support: Barriers and Bridges*. Department of Social Security Research Report No. 53. London: HMSO

Shaw, M., Dorling, D., Gordon, D. and Davey Smith, G. (1999) *The Widening Gap: Health Inequalities and Policy in Britain*. Bristol: The Policy Press

Sinclair, I. and Gibbs, I. (2002) 'Looked after children', in J. Bradshaw (ed.) *The Well-being of Children in the UK*. London: Save the Children

Skinner, C. (2003) *Running around in Circles: Coordinating Childcare Education and Work*. Bristol: Policy Press

Sloane, P.J. and Theodossiou, I. (1996) 'Earnings mobility, family income and low pay', *The Economic Journal*, Vol. 106, pp. 657–66

Smeaton, D. and McKay, S. (2003) *Working after State Pension Age: Quantitative Analysis*. DWP Research Report No. 182. http://www.dwp.gov.uk/asd/asd5/rrep182.html (site visited May 2003)

Smith, T. and Noble, M. (1995) *Education Divides: Poverty and Schooling in the 1990s*. London: CPAG.

Social Exclusion Unit (2002a) *National Strategy for Neighbourhood Renewal. Report of Policy Action Team 12: Young People*. London: Social Exclusion Unit

Social Exclusion Unit (2002b) *Young Runaways*. London: Social Exclusion Unit

Social Security Select Committee (2000) *Pensioner Poverty, Seventh Report*. London: House of Commons

Stewart, M.B. (1998) 'Low pay, no pay dynamics', in J. Hills (ed.) *Persistent Poverty and Lifetime Inequality*. London: Centre for the Analysis of Social Exclusion, LSE and HM Treasury

Stewart, M.B. (1999) 'Low pay in Britain', in P. Gregg and J. Wadsworth (eds) *The State of Working Britain*. Manchester: Manchester University Press

Stewart, M.B. and Swaffield, J.K. (1999) 'Low pay dynamics and transition probabilities', *Economica*, Vol. 66, pp. 23–42

Sutherland, H. (2001) *Five Labour Budgets (1997–2001): Impact on the Distribution of Household Income and on Child Poverty*. Microsimulation Unit Research Note No. 41

Sutherland, H. (2002) *One Parent Families, Poverty and Labour Policy*. London: National Council for One Parent Families

Sutherland, H., Sefton, T. and Piachaud, D. (2003) *Poverty in Britain: The Impact of Government Policy since 1997*. York: Joseph Rowntree Foundation

Tabberer, S., Hall, C., Pendergast, S. and Webster, A. (2000) *Teenage Pregnancy and Choice. Abortion or Motherhood: Influences on the Decision*. York: Joseph Rowntree Foundation, York

Treolar, P. (2002) 'New tax credits: will they tackle child poverty?', *Poverty*, Vol. 12

Turok, I. and Edge, N. (1999) *The Jobs Gap in Britain's Cities: Employment Loss and Labour Market Consequences.* Bristol: The Policy Press

UNICEF Innocenti Research Centre (2000) *A League Table of Child Poverty in Rich Nations.* Innocenti Report Card, No. 1. London: UNICEF Innocenti Research Centre

Utting, W. (1997) *People Like Us: Report of the Review of Safeguards for Children Living away from Home.* London: Department of Health and the Welsh Office

Van Drenth, A., Knijn, T. and Lewis, J. (1999) 'Sources of income for lone mother families: policy changes in Britain and the Netherlands and the experiences of divorced women', *Journal of Social Policy*, Vol. 28, No. 4, pp. 619–41

Vegeris, S. and McKay, S. (2002) *Low/moderate-income Families in Britain: Changes in Living Standards 1999—2000.* DWP Research Report 164. Leeds: Corporate Document Services

Walker, A., Maher, J., Coulthard, M., Goddard, E. and Thomas, M. (2001) *Living in Britain: Results from the 2000/01 General Household Survey, National Statistics.* London: The Stationery Office

Walker, R. (1998a) 'New tools: towards a dynamic science of modern society', in L. Leisering and R. Walker (eds) *The Dynamics of Modern Society.* Bristol: The Policy Press

Walker, R. (1998b) 'Escaping from social assistance in Great Britain', in L. Leisering and R. Walker (eds) *The Dynamics of Modern Society.* Bristol: The Policy Press

Walker, R. and Ashworth, K. (1994) *Poverty Dynamics: Issues and Examples.* Aldershot: Avebury

Webb, S., Kemp, M. and Millar, J. (1996) 'The changing face of low pay in Britain', *Policy Studies*, Vol. 17, No. 4, pp. 255–71

Webster, D. (2000) 'The geographical concentration of labour-market disadvantage', *Oxford Review of Economic Policy*, Vol. 16, pp. 114–28

Willitts, M. and Swales, K. (2003) *Characteristics of Large Families.* London: HMSO

Zaidi, A. (2001) *Snakes and Ladders: An Analysis of Life-course Events and Income Mobility in Old Age.* ESRC-SAGE Discussion Paper No. 8. London: London School of Economics. http://www.lse.ac.uk/Depts/sage/pdf/SAGE_DP8.pdf (site visited May 2003)

Zaidi, A., Rake, K. and Falkingham, J. (2001) *Income Mobility in Later Life.* ESRC-SAGE Discussion Paper No. 3. London: London School of Economics. http://www.lse.ac.uk/Depts/sage/pdf/SAGE_DP3.pdf (site visited May 2003)